# Beloved Children

## A 40-day Devotional

Lorraine Dittrich

# Beloved Children

Copyright © 2025 Lorraine Dittrich

First edition published 2025

The moral right of the author to full ownership of the copyright of *Beloved Children* has been asserted. All rights are reserved. The book may not be reproduced in part or whole without prior written permission from the author.

| | |
|---|---|
| Editing by: | Anna Cullen |
| | annas.editing.int@gmail.com |
| Cover & Interior Design by: | WordWyze Publishing |
| | wordwyze.nz |

Copies of *Beloved Children* are available in New Zealand to be purchased direct from the author who can be contacted by email (address at the back of the book under the Author's Note).

All scripture quotations taken from The Holy Bible, English Standard Version®, copyright © 2001 by Crossway Bibles, a publishing ministry of Good News Publishers. Used by permission, www.esv.org.

International POD through IngramSpark

A catalogue record for this book is available from the National Library of New Zealand.

**Paperback ISBN:**    978-0-473-76578-1

# Contents

Acknowledgements .................................................................. vi
1 Like Children ........................................................................ 9
2 Only the Body .................................................................... 11
3 All-Knowing ....................................................................... 13
4 No Way Out ....................................................................... 15
5 Being Set Apart ................................................................. 17
6 Prayer Works ..................................................................... 19
7 Take Refuge ...................................................................... 21
8 Work With Him or For Him ............................................... 23
9 Cannot Wait ...................................................................... 25
10 Faith and Trust ................................................................ 27
11 The Letter Kills ................................................................ 29
12 Gifts ................................................................................. 31
13 Visualise Answered Prayer ............................................. 33
14 Believe Half and Half-Not ............................................... 35
15 For His Own Pleasure ..................................................... 37
16 A Big Yes .......................................................................... 39
17 Faith Like a Marshmallow .............................................. 41
18 It is My Life ...................................................................... 43
19 Unconditional Love ......................................................... 45
20 Make Peace With ............................................................ 47
21 The Good Soil .................................................................. 49
22 Imprisonment .................................................................. 51
23 What If? ........................................................................... 53
24 A Blend of Life and Faith ................................................ 55
25 Be Yourself ...................................................................... 57

| | |
|---|---|
| 26 The Devil is Gone, But… | 59 |
| 27 God the Creator | 61 |
| 28 God Listens | 63 |
| 29 Jesus is Light | 65 |
| 30 Hiding from God | 67 |
| 31 Good People | 69 |
| 32 Going to Hell | 71 |
| 33 Receptive Minds | 73 |
| 34 What is your Reality? | 75 |
| 35 Rejoice | 77 |
| 36 Words and Actions | 79 |
| 37 Favouritism | 81 |
| 38 Discipline versus Punishment | 83 |
| 39 Keeps on Escaping | 85 |
| 40 No Grandchildren | 87 |
| THE AUTHOR'S NOTES | 89 |

Dedicated to my children,
my grandchildren, and
all the children who crossed my path
throughout the past fifty-six years.

# Acknowledgements

A heartfelt thank you to the following persons:

Pastor Erik Stolte, from the Reformed Church currently in Pukekohe. His encouragement at the beginning of this journey meant a lot. Erik's comments on the first twenty devotions assured me I was moving in the right direction.

Pastor Sjirk Bajema was of great help regarding the theological aspects and his comments after a quick proofreading of some devotions. His encouragement meant a lot.

John van Dijk, the editor of our congregation's weekly Bulletin, is skilled in the art of writing and was the key in leading me to view the contents with fresh eyes.

Then there is Natalie Amersfoort, my clever granddaughter. An essay writer to be reckoned with. She edited the first twenty devotions and helped me tremendously by suggesting the correct grammatical aspects.

Marise Rossouw kindly edited the second twenty devotions, and was at the time completing her degree in English. Her knowledge of the English language was very helpful.

I owe great gratitude to Colleen Kaluza from Wordwyze. From the first contact, I knew I had discovered a professional regarding all aspects of getting my book print-ready. All my anxiety and fears about finding my way to self-publish disappeared. She was knowledgeable and greatly supportive. I knew instantly this new venture in writing my first book was going to end well.

Last, this book would never have happened if it were not for all the wonderful Christians who crossed my path throughout my life. They taught me what love is, starting with their love for God, which manifested in their daily walk and interaction with others. A love that touched all those around them, young and old. Only God could provide this kind of love.

Soli Deo Gloria. Glory to God alone.

"Let the little children come to me;
and do not hinder them,
for to such belongs the kingdom of heaven.
Truly, I say to you, whoever does not
receive the kingdom of God like a child
shall not enter it."
Mark 10:14-15


"Whoever humbles himself like this child
is the greatest in the kingdom of heaven."
Matthew 18:4


"… he gave the right to become children of God, who were born,
not of blood nor of the will of the flesh,
nor of the will of man, but of God."
John 1:12-13


"Therefore be imitators of God as beloved children.
And walk in love, as Christ loved us
and gave himself up for us,
A fragrant offering and sacrifice to God."
Ephesians 5:1-2

# 1
# Like Children

"Mummy, I wish I could die…"

Before expressing my shock, our four-year-old added, "…because then I could sit on Jesus' lap and ask Him all the questions I don't know the answers to."

Her remark intrigued me. What kind of questions would a four-year-old have? Maybe she didn't even know herself. Perhaps she already sensed at that tender age that whatever confused her about her small world, she could share with Him. To her, the only way to find the answers she sought would be if she could meet Him face to face.

We are all like children, seeking answers. Children always ask questions and often wear parents out with their persistence. We act in the same way – while not always verbalising our thoughts, we carry these questions within. The uncertainty of the world leads us to confusion, which leads to a desire and urgency to find answers we believe will enable us to cope.

Answers to our questions give security, make us feel assured things are under control and, above all, bring hope for a better future. That is, if someone provides us with answers from a reliable source we can trust. Children accept answers if they feel loved and secured by the person who gives them. The truthfulness of the answers makes processing information so much easier. This applies to young and old.

Unfortunately, the answers to their questions can disillusion both adults and children. In the adult world, there are a wide range of sources to finding answers to global warming, health issues, political situations, and religion. There are also many questions regarding personal matters. But information and explanations are forever changing, and lead to more questions and more confusion.

But do we need to find an answer regarding every issue? Imagine the joy of having one source we can wholeheartedly trust! A source that will provide insight and put this world and our own lives in perspective. Someone who will not only provide answers but will lead us to find meaning in our existence, giving us hope for the here and now and for everlasting life. That could make life so much simpler and worth living. A person in whom all the questions become one answer.

There is such a source – God as Trinity, who created all living things in heaven and on earth. He possesses perfect knowledge of His creation. God is All-Knowing. We can trust Him with the work of His hands, of which we are the crown (Psalm 8). He is also our Father who loves us with an immeasurable love, confirmed in 1 John 3:1, "See what kind of love the father has given to us, that we should be called children of God; and so we are." It will be foolish to doubt His love, "For God so loved the world, that he gave his only Son, that whoever believes in him should not perish but have eternal life." (John 3:16)

The above Scripture shows us our place in this world, created by God, loved by Him as His children, and given eternal life by His Son. But how do we know how to live in this world? This knowledge comes from the Holy Spirit, who we receive through faith. This is the promise, "He will guide you into all the truth." (John 16:13)

When we seek God with all our hearts in prayer and with the opened Bible in our hands daily, we will always find the answers we seek. In this tumultuous world God acts on our behalf, "From of old no one has heard or perceived by the ear, no one has seen a God besides you, who acts for those who wait for him." (Isaiah 64:4)

**REFLECTION: Psalm 62:5-8**

# 2
# Only the Body

While washing the dishes, my eye caught through the kitchen window our eldest son running as fast as a five-year-old's legs could carry him. It intrigued me because no one was chasing after him. He stopped, turned around, and aimed his wooden gun at an unseen enemy. He said something, took a step closer as though challenged by the enemy, dropped his toy gun and fell to the ground, acting like he was dead.

Later, during lunch, my curiosity got the better of me, and I asked my son about his game. His answer was very unexpected.

"The Russians were chasing me. They wanted to kill me. I tried to get away from them, but I couldn't. I knew they wanted to kill me."

That the enemy was a Russian was no surprise because South Africa, where we lived at the time, had sent troops to Angola to help against the Russian invasion a year or two before.

"Then I remembered what you said, Mummy."

"And what was that?" I asked.

"You said that when we love Jesus, nothing can take that love away. Remember, Mummy, I asked you if death could take it away, and you said, 'No, even when we die, that love will go with us into heaven'."

Surprised that he remembered so well, I asked what he said to the 'Russian' who wanted to kill him.

"I said to him he could kill my body, and that's okay, but my heart will go to Jesus full of love for Him."

He did not realise the impact it had on me to hear about the trust he put in the unseen God, even while *staring death in the face*. Though it was just a game, I knew how real games were for children.

Today, followers of Christ still die worldwide because of their faith. The big question we must ask ourselves is, "What will I choose when facing death because of my faith?" Is my faith the most important factor in my life? Do I put it above my life and that of my family? Would denouncing Jesus comes easy?

If there is any hesitation in answering these questions, we should earnestly ask the Lord to show us what we lack in our faith and trust in Him. Matthew 10:28 says: "And do not fear those who kill the body but cannot kill the soul. Rather, fear Him who can destroy both soul and body in hell."

Let us pray that the wicked never persecute us, putting us in a position where we must choose between Christ and our own lives or the lives of our loved ones. But whatever may await us on such a day, may we say with all our hearts: "The Lord is on my side; I will not fear. What can man do to me?" (Psalm 118:6). Let us take solace in the promise in Luke 12:12, "for the Holy Spirit will teach you in that very hour what you ought to say."

**REFLECTION: John 15:18-26**

# 3
# All-Knowing

It was late, and I wanted to get to bed as soon as I tucked the girls in. I gave each a quick kiss. But as I was about to put off the light, one of my girls called out.

"Mummy, why didn't God stop Eve from eating the fruit from the tree in the middle of the garden? You said He knows everything; He should have known beforehand that Eve and Adam would eat from the forbidden fruit. If He stopped them, we would not have such a hard time here on earth."

I sighed. I didn't have the energy to explain such a profound theological question. But I also realised that this moment would pass, and I may lose the opportunity to answer her question. Are parents not commanded in the Bible to instruct their children in the truth?

So, I said a quick prayer in my heart, asking for wisdom and the mental energy to answer her question as well as I could. Sitting on the side of her bed, I explained that God never intended us to be puppets. I could see that I had her full attention with that remark – she loved puppet shows. I asked, "What do you like the most about a puppet show?" She remarked, "I can make them do and say anything I want them to."

God made us in His own image, and as part of this He gave us a free will. Unlike puppets, we can make our own choices. From the moment we wake up, we choose what time to get up, what clothes to wear, what kind of breakfast we would like to eat, and so on. We also choose whom to like and even love, obey, and what rules to follow.

Though God knows everything, He wanted Adam and Eve to obey Him out of their own free will. In the same way, He does not force us. He does not force us to love Him and follow Him. To this day, it is our decision.

Adam and Eve made the wrong decision and listened to the serpent. Their disobedience led to consequences that affected the entire human race. God warned them, but they still followed their own way.

Our girl with the questioning mind was falling asleep by now. But sleep didn't come easy for me that night. I could not help thinking about the brokenness of this world caused by Adam and Eve's sin of disobedience.

However, our All-Knowing God had another plan in place. He is love; therefore, He did not plan to abandon Adam and Eve and the rest of humankind with them. Though He banished Adam and Eve from the Garden of Eden, He did not turn his grace away from them. When Adam and Eve discovered they were naked, God's grace already covered them. He sent them away, clothed in the skin of a slaughtered animal. This foretold that the blood of Christ would cover us in His grace and set us free from Adam and Eve's disobedience (Genesis 3:1-24).

Thank God for the first promise He made with the fall of Adam and Eve. Jesus would have victory over the serpent: "...he shall bruise your head, and you shall bruise his heel." (Genesis 3:15b)

This fulfilment of His promise on the cross changed the grave decision of Adam and Eve into the most gracious blessing for those that believe.

**REFLECTION: Romans 3:21-26**

_____
_____
_____
_____
_____
_____
_____

# 4
# No Way Out

I was concentrating on the late afternoon traffic with my younger daughter in the back seat. I did not notice that she was less talkative than usual. It had been stressful the past few days, and I felt worn out.

Earlier, we had rushed her sister to hospital with a life-threatening brain infection called encephalitis. The 300 kilometres from our small rural town to the city felt never-ending. All my husband and I could think about was getting medical care for her as soon as possible. We had no option but to take her younger five-year-old sister with us – there was no time to arrange a childminder.

Now, on the way to our hotel, my five-year-old spoke for the first time since we left the hospital.

"Not being at home makes me feel like a little girl lost in a forest. There is just no path that will take me out of this forest. Please take me home, Mummy. It is okay if you leave me there with someone. If I don't get home soon, I will be like a flower wilting, losing a petal each day."

Her description left me without words. Could a five-year-old express her feelings in metaphors like these? We picked up already that she could express herself very well and showed excellent language skills, but these remarks were exceptional.

Recalling this incident many years later reminded me of times in my life and other people's lives when experiencing various trials. Times of trials, hardships, loss, and grief create a dark forest, or rather a wilderness, not only surrounding us through an unbearable situation, but often within as well. In times like these, we feel lost and without a way out.

The Bible has many examples of wilderness times in people's lives.

Jacob told a lie to his father, Isaac, pretending he was his brother Esau, and receiving the blessing meant for him. For many years, the brothers could not find a way out of the wilderness of their past and the resentment it caused (Genesis 27:42-45).

Then there is David, pursued by Saul relentlessly. David had to seek paths that could lead him away from Saul and out of harm's way, often hiding in the wilderness. The psalms of David give account of him and his spiritual wilderness, often because of Saul, but there was also the sin he committed with Bathsheba, and his grief over his son Absolom's behaviour (Psalm 51, 2 Samuel 13:30-33).

Times in the wilderness always serve a purpose. A good example is the Jews in the time of Moses. The Jews spent 40 years trapped in the wilderness before they could enter the Promised Land. During that time, they learned to trust the Lord and His plans. They learned perseverance and that life could still go on. It was bearable because they knew there was a set time for their suffering to end. Even though only their children and the generations to follow would enter the Promised Land, they found it enough to know that God would fulfil His promise (Joshua 5:6).

During our 'wilderness' times, may we trust the Lord and his plans, and may this fill us with hope, knowing that the Lord allows such times for us to strengthen our faith. "'For I know what plans I have for you,' declares the Lord, 'plans for welfare and not for evil, to give you a future and hope.'" (Jeremiah 29:11)

**REFLECTION: Genesis 50:15-21; James 1:2-7**

# 5
# Being Set Apart

I was tidying up the playroom at the kindergarten after all the children had gone home when I was called to the phone. I recognised the voice as the mother of one of the five-year-old boys in my group.

"Hello, Lorraine, what on earth have you told my son today? When I dropped him off this morning, he was keen to get a haircut this afternoon. But he bawled out his eyes and refused to go to the hairdresser when I picked him up. He said he would never have a haircut again because it would make him weak."

I realised where that had come from. Earlier, I told the children the story of Samson and Delilah (Judges 16). Unfortunately, I have quite a flair for the dramatic and had gone a bit too far in retelling this epic tale.

After I talked to this serious little fellow on the phone and explained that Samson was an exception and that there had never again been anyone to whom God gave that kind of strength, all was well and he got his haircut.

God set apart Samson to be a Nazarite. A Nazarite was someone who took a vow, consecrating himself to be sacred (Numbers 6:1-5). He was obliged to abstain from wine, and a razor could never touch his hair during his lifetime.

What made Samson different from other Nazarites was that God gifted him with extreme strength. He received this strength to defeat the Philistines and free the Jews from their oppression.

Sadly, Samson ignored God's commands, which included not touching any deceased creature. He ate honey from the carcass of a lion (Judges 14:8). Then there was his marriage to a woman from the enemy camp. But the last step in his moral decline was when he got involved with the prostitute, Delilah. He became weak in spirit when she deceived him. He gave in to avoid her nagging, and told her the secret to his strength. Delilah cut Samson's hair, causing him to lose his strength. Losing his extreme strength allowed Samson to fall into the hands of the enemy (Judges 16).

Our acceptance by faith of Jesus as our Saviour makes us spiritual Nazarites, set apart for His kingdom. God looks upon us as holy, sacred to Him. He calls us saints at various times in the Bible. "Love the Lord, all you, his saints!" (Psalm 31:23a), is but one example.

Do we think and act as set apart? Though we have not received extreme physical strength, we have received another special gift: power from the Holy Spirit. Therefore, we have the strength to overcome temptations that lead to sin. We should acknowledge the power of the Holy Spirit in humbleness, use it wisely, be aware of its continuous presence, and draw upon it in prayer.

Psalm 31:23 continues by assuring and warning those set apart by faith that "The Lord preserves the faithful but abundantly repays those who act with pride."

Let us learn from Samson that pride leads to weakness. In Samson's case, it was his physical strength that he took pride in, as though it was by his own doing.

No, let us rather remember that "His divine power has granted to us all things that pertain to life and godliness, through the knowledge of him who called us to his own glory and excellence." (2 Peter 1:3)

**REFLECTION: Jeremiah 9:23-24**

_____
_____
_____
_____
_____
_____
_____

# 6
# Prayer Works

I looked at the faces before me, reading intense anxiety in the eyes of our children.

"Mum, do you think Mathew will be okay, and that he will see again?"

I groaned inwardly. How was I going to break the news that Mathew, our beloved tabby cat, was going to be put down, or perhaps was already gone?

Earlier that day, I noticed him bumping into furniture and trying to find his water bowl. I immediately took him to the vet, where I learned he had become blind. The vet concluded a car had hit him earlier that day. The best way was to put him down, the vet suggested. We left Mathew with him. That was early evening. Now, close to bedtime, the children wanted to be reassured. I didn't have the heart to tell them the truth. Tomorrow, yes, but not tonight.

"Well, let's pray the Lord will heal him," suggested my son, who took his role as big brother seriously.

The girls closed their eyes and waited for their brother to take the lead. Each of them took a turn, asking the Lord, or rather pleading with Him, to heal Mathew.

Much more at peace with the situation, they went to bed. I, however, did not sleep, knowing that Matt was already no more, as the vet had planned the procedure for that evening.

Early the next morning, the phone rang, and when I heard the vet's voice, my heart missed a beat. I dreaded him asking me to collect our much-loved cat's body. But to my astonishment, the vet sounded very cheery.

"Good news, Lorraine. Matt was fine this morning. He had fully regained his sight. You must thank my wife. I already had the syringe in my hand, ready to put him down, when my wife entered the room and stopped me from using it. She asked if we could wait till this morning to see what might happen overnight."

The news delighted the children, and the first thing our son said was, "See, prayer works!" In childlike faith, they prayed in the certainty that the Lord would hear their prayer.

We should maintain the childlike aspect of our faith and believe that our prayers will be answered. "Therefore, I tell you, whatever you ask in prayer, believe that you have received it, and it will be yours." (Mark 11:24)

Other aspects which underlie our prayer life include a realisation of our dependency on the Lord to help us, and an acknowledgment of our own feebleness and weakness. Seeking Him in His Word and following His commands will cultivate a desire to pray continuously. Even in between the busy moments of our lives. John 15:7 provides the promise, "If you abide in me, and my words abide in you, ask whatever you wish, and it will be done for you."

There is also the following assurance, "And this is the confidence that we have toward him, that if we ask anything according to His will, He hears us." (1 John 5:14)

The Lord hears our prayers – isn't that enough reason to rejoice? For the answers may differ from what we expected, but it would prove to be the best answer. "Rejoice always, pray without ceasing, give thanks in all circumstances; for this is the will of God in Christ Jesus for you." (1 Thessalonians 5:16-18)

**REFLECTION: Mark 11:20-25**

_____
_____
_____
_____
_____

# 7
# Take Refuge

After we moved from the city to a small rural town in northwest South Africa, I finished my postgraduate studies in pre-primary teaching. I started a kindergarten to practise my newfound knowledge and benefit our two young daughters. Premises were hard to find, so with the help of my husband we changed the double garage into a playroom. The double carport was ideal for providing more space for pre-school activities, and it proved to be welcomed by parents. Soon enough, there was a waiting list.

Our younger girl, quite a sensitive child, started disappearing sometimes. The first time it happened, our cleaner looked everywhere for her. To her surprise, she found the girl under the mulberry bush, sitting against the trunk, whispering to herself. The low-hanging branches and greenery well hid her from sight.

When I asked her about this, she explained, "It is so noisy with all these children around. Nothing feels the same anymore, Mummy. I just want to be alone, away from it all. That is why I am hiding there."

As young as she was, she realised that sometimes when things get too much to cope with, you must remove yourself from the situation and go into hiding.

Avoidance is also loving your neighbour, because being frustrated and annoyed by their actions often leads to sinning against them in your mind. Negative thoughts can lead to anger and aggression.

I am sure we have all experienced times when we felt like running away from the present, being over committed to specific causes, duties, and responsibilities. Often, we feel trapped or squeezed into a corner.

We all need a safe place to retreat or take refuge from hectic everyday lives. Voices surround us non-stop through social media and entertainment channels. Even our own voices penetrate the so-called quiet moments with anxious self-talk.

Do we need a tree to hide under? Even if we had one, whatever form or shape it may have, will it help in the long run? There are different *'trees'* we use to get away from it all, such as shopping sprees, spending time in the gym, running or walking for kilometres on end, and many other pursuits. Nothing is wrong with these, but do they give us the quietness of spirit that we seek?

But praise the Lord! He offers Himself as our refuge. David must have experienced this firsthand. David sought many quiet places to hide from Saul's pursuit. During those times, David found God as his refuge and help (Psalm 46:1). One of these quiet places was a cave in the wilderness, En-Gedi, where he wrote the beautiful Psalm 57.

We cannot retreat to a quiet place without being assured it will lead us to prayer. If we seek the Lord in all sincerity, we will find Him in the stillness of that quiet place.

We need His mercy throughout our lives, but to experience it in its fullness, we need to seek Him as our refuge, our *Tree*. May our prayer be, "Be merciful to me, O God, be merciful to me, for in you my soul takes refuge, in the shadow of your wings I will take refuge…." (Psalm 57:1)

When we add to our *Tree,* the substance of His Word, it will fill us with joy, making us ready to face whoever and whatever we are hiding from. "But let all who take refuge in you rejoice; let them ever sing for joy, and spread your protection over them, that those who love your name may exult in you." (Psalm 5:11)

**REFLECTION: Psalm 57**

_____
_____
_____
_____
_____
_____

# 8
# Work With Him or For Him

All children enjoy spending time alone with their parents without having siblings around. Our son was no exception. Our town was remote, meaning we often had to travel long distances to sports games and cultural events, journeys which provided the perfect opportunity for this valuable one-on-one time.

On one of these trips, my son and I were discussing career choices. He didn't need to make subject choices yet as he was only in intermediate, but I found it interesting to hear about his dreams for the future. So, I asked him about that.

He answered by saying that he would like to become a preacher. When I asked what led him to choose this vocation, his answer was surprising: "I want to work every day for the Lord. I can't imagine not being busy with the Lord's things all my life."

I applauded him for his vision for the future, but I felt it was important to point out that he didn't need to become a preacher to work every day for the Lord. As believers, we should have a daily desire to focus on the things of the Lord, which originate from our love for Him.

But what are the things of the Lord? Believers often separate Jesus and their faith from other aspects of their everyday lives, but they should interweave with each other. It is important to do everyday activities, including chores and even the mundane, joyfully. Seeking God's hand in it. "Whatever you do, work heartily, as for the Lord and not for men, knowing that from the Lord you will receive the inheritance as your reward." (Colossians 3:23-24)

So, whatever the task, we are told to do it wholeheartedly because our work is ultimately not for the praise, acknowledgment, and appreciation we will receive from our family and friends, or even the wages from the boss. No, an inheritance awaits us in its own time from the Lord.

But there lies a hidden danger in interpreting Paul's words. We must be careful not to become obsessive in our work for the Lord, trying to convince ourselves that all our involvement in church groups, charities, and doing good, is to serve the Lord. The underlying danger is thinking that the more exhausted we are after a day's *doing-good* activities, the greater our commitment to the Lord is. This mindset often leads to the state of being so busy with the things of the Lord that there is no time left for the Lord of the things. The last part of Colossians 3:23-24 puts it into perspective, "You are serving the Lord Christ." So, therefore, the tasks at hand must not overshadow our focus on the Master we serve.

We must also guard against the aspect of *Self* and remind ourselves that we must work with Him. When we work with Him, we will pray for His guidance and ask where and how He wants us to serve.

I've experienced disappointment in the past when I've seen a need and wanted to jump in and help, only to discover someone else had already done so. I needed to learn that the Lord answered my prayer to help others, but did not appoint the role of 'helper' to me in every situation.

We can do many good things for others by serving Him. Let us pray for His guidance to lead us in the tasks He has set aside for us to bless our fellowmen. "For we are His workmanship, created in Christ Jesus for good works, which God prepared beforehand, that we should walk in them." (Ephesians 2:10)

**REFLECTION: John 13:12-17**

# 9
# Cannot Wait

After we arrived in our new town, I received the shocking news that a school friend of mine had died in a car accident some years before our arrival. She had married a farmer in that area, and I was looking forward to catching up with her. Unfortunately, we had lost contact entirely after school, and now it was too late.

One afternoon, I visited my deceased friend's grave. I had to take our girls and their friend with me, and thought that introducing them to a cemetery could be a good idea and might have some educational value.

The inscription on the headstone of my friend was beautiful. It says, 'Her life was a Psalm'.

As I read this aloud, they wanted to know what it meant. I explained a psalm is a holy song. My friend believed in God and so her life was like a holy song. I told them how delighted her husband and family were that she was in heaven with Jesus.

Then they wanted to know how heaven looked. I painted it as the Bible does; it is a place like no other – beautiful, where there is no crying, weeping, sadness or wrongdoing. There is perfect peace and happiness.

On our way back to the car, I noticed raised voices behind me. I stopped and turned around to see three agitated little faces glaring at each other.

I asked what was wrong, and one of my girls answered, "Mummy, I want to go to heaven first, but *he* wants to go first," pointing to her friend. These two six-year-olds looked as if they were going to get physical. But then the five-year-old yelled, "Stop, stop! I want to go first."

This incident made me smile and touched me. Though it was such a childlike view of death, there was a message in it.

Why do so many of us fear death? I think the answer lies in how we view our lives on earth, for this is the only reality for now. We push death and heaven to the back of our minds. It is a daily struggle just to get through the present. The future holds the dreams of what we still want to achieve. Our ultimate end of being with the Lord becomes too distant because of the unknown it holds.

The Bible teaches that death is an inevitable part of life. Life starts with birth and ends in physical death. Above all, the Bible teaches that death has not got the final say. Life on this earth is only temporary. "All flesh is like grass and all its glory like the flower of grass. The grass withers and the flower falls, but the word of the Lord remains forever." (1 Peter 1:24-25)

But can we face death without fear? David gives us the assurance in Psalm 23:4, "Even though I walk through the valley of the shadow of death, I will fear no evil, for you are with me; your rod and your staff, they comfort me." The Lord will be right there when we utter our last breath. He will be alongside us when he leads and takes us Home.

May we have a sure hope for what awaits us. Jesus had victory over death on our behalf on the cross. He removed the sting of death, which is sin. We should live in agreement with what Paul wrote in 1 Corinthians 15:55, "Death is swallowed up in victory. O death, where is your victory? O death, where is your sting?"

In the meantime, we can live this life well by glorifying God in this present reality – life on earth. Knowing that an unimaginable reality beyond description is awaiting us in the life to come.

**REFLECTION: Hebrews 12:22-29**

_____
_____
_____
_____
_____
_____
_____

# 10
# Faith and Trust

One morning, as I welcomed the pre-schoolers, one mother asked if she could talk to me. She had worried as she watched her son pick at his breakfast that morning. She also said her son had stopped drinking milk, his favourite drink, and was only drinking water.

I recognised the reason behind his refusal. The story of Daniel, which I had shared with the children a couple of days ago, must have affected this boy who took it too literally. I assured the mother that I would handle the situation with wisdom. I explained to the boy why Daniel and his friends chose such a diet. I emphasised it was relevant for their position back then but did not apply to us today.

In the first chapter of his book, Daniel informs the reader where he stood in his relationship with God. His and his friends' refusal to enjoy the same food as the Babylonian King's court showed their allegiance to God. They showed that their loyalty was not to any earthly king, and that king Nebuchadnezzar and the Babylonians worshipped idols. That made it impossible for Daniel and his three friends to enjoy the delicacies offered to them in the palace. The custom was that a portion of the food and wine would be offered to the gods before the king would eat. Daniel and his friends' refusal to share the same food as the king protected them from being part of this idolatry.

They had no fear of the consequences of their decision. They feared God more than any human being, regardless of that person's status or position.

Not much has changed since this account in Daniel 1. Idolaters who worship earthly pleasures surround us still today, their delicacies served on lavish entertainment platters. Often, we make efforts to accommodate all those who have non-Christian views, even pretending to go along because we don't want to be seen as the odd ones out.

Why is it so hard to stand out in a world that serves delicacies that are tasteless without the Lord? I think Daniel and his friends showed us the answer. They did not fear the potential consequences of their request to have only vegetables and water for ten days (Daniel 1:12). They believed with all their hearts in the Lord's power above any other. Previous generations passed the account of God's mighty hand in the history of the Jews on to them. They knew nothing was impossible for God.

They trusted Him and had faith that the Lord would bless them for this decision. And He did. "At the end of ten days it was seen that they were better in appearance and fatter in the flesh than all the youths who ate the king's food." (Daniel 1:15)

The Lord blessed them not only physically but also spiritually and mentally. "As for these four youths, God gave them learning and skill in all literature and wisdom, and Daniel had understanding in all visions and dreams." (Daniel 1:17)

If only we could trust and believe like Daniel and his friends, regardless of pressure to conform and answer to others' worldly expectations. If we could look past the heavy-laden table of delicacies of this world, and turn rather to the water and bread that satisfy our spiritual hunger in such a way that we will never thirst or hunger again, Jesus promises that what He offers outweighs anything the world ever can entice us with: "The water I will give him will become in him a spring of water welling up to eternal life" and "I am the bread of life." (John 4:14 and John 6:35)

## REFLECTION: John 6:26-40

# 11
# The Letter Kills

In my second year of teaching, I got a position at a primary school close to where my parents lived. My first year had taught me that independence in the big city of Johannesburg could be a lonely path. I was looking forward to teaching at a school in a rural town. The upper-middle-class suburb was a complete contrast to my previous school, where the children were sometimes neglected and impoverished.

Every morning, my Year Four students greeted me with sparkling eyes and eager faces. They could not wait to see what I would teach them that day. I faced more pressure than I expected and had to strive to live up to their lofty expectations.

One morning during the Bible lesson, I was relating the story of the ten plagues. I told the class about Pharaoh, and was concentrating so hard on the content that I did not realise I was referring to Pharaoh as 'King Pharaoh'.

A hand shot up from a delightful girl at the back of the class. I nodded in her direction for a response.

"Miss, it is not king Pharoah, but only Pharoah because the word Pharoah means king. So, what you are saying right now is, king-king."

I thanked her for the correction. I had the urge to defend myself but remembered that one of our lecturers said we must be big enough of heart to accept correction. Even criticism from our students.

The insight of the girl surprised me. She was bold enough to speak up, valuing accuracy even in the face of potential discomfort.

As time passed, I realised how important reading with perception is, now more than ever. Many Christians make it their mission to read the whole Bible as many times as possible in their lifetime. There is nothing wrong with such a desire. But the danger is that it becomes an exercise in enriching the mind with facts alone. These readers are significant assets to teams taking part in Bible quizzes. They are also often those who spend much time on lengthy debates by arguing aspects of the Word. Sometimes, when you mention the spiritual side of the Bible and aspects of faith, you may find little depth and insight from those avid Bible readers.

It's fine to read the Bible from start to finish as many times as we want, but without studying the content, we're only skimming the surface. The secret lies in the goal. Is it about gaining knowledge only, or growing in knowing who God is and what it means for you spiritually? The latter will lead to what the author of Proverbs describes: "For wisdom will come into your heart, and knowledge will be pleasant to your soul; discretion will watch over you, understanding will guard you." (Proverbs 2:10-11)

If we long to achieve this goal as we grow in our faith, we need to pray for the guidance and teaching of the Holy Spirit every time we open the Bible to read and study it. The input of the Spirit in exploring the Bible will protect us from focusing only on the letter, the consequences of which Paul warns us against in 2 Corinthians 3:6, "For the letter kills, but the Spirit gives life."

May the Word delight us greatly and nurture our desire to meditate upon it day and night, as the Psalmist often encourages us to do. "I rise before dawn and cry for help; I hope in your words. My eyes are awake before the watches of the night, that I may meditate on your promise." (Psalm 119:147-148)

**REFLECTION: 2 Corinthians 4:1-6**

# 12
# Gifts

I once read that by watching children play, you can get glimpses of their gifts and can almost predict what they will become over time as those gifts develop.

One girl stands out in my memory of those early kindergarten days. She was smaller in build than her peers. Her dark, almost black eyes were very observant, and I got the impression she had a self-awareness exceeding that of her peers. Although she was not talkative, her eyes assured me that much was happening inside her young mind. Her mother remarked that this girl could repeat the day's events in the smallest detail and had such a colourful way with words that the family looked forward to her storytelling every evening. Many years later, she became a well-known bestselling South African author and received many awards.

Discovering our gifts may be a lifelong journey. Sometimes people confuse interest with a specific gift. You may have an interest in painting but may not be a gifted painter. Others may recognise our gifts, yet we may be in denial of them, perhaps fearing the hard work it may take to bring the gift to fruition, or because of a lack of confidence. Often, the fear of failure prevents us from pursuing our gifts.

Whatever the case may be, one fact remains in that the Lord, as our Creator, equipped us with at least one gift each. As believers, instead of being too humble by saying, "I have no gift," we should pray and ask the Lord to show us how we can serve Him most effectively with the gift He has given us. If we struggle to recognise our gift, He will reveal it to us as we seek an answer through prayer. Sometimes, His answer is to make us aware of a desire we buried away long ago.

Often, we may not recognise something that comes naturally to us as a gift. Part of any gift is a desire to put it into motion. The Lord always opens doors and paves the way for you to put that desire to use for the good of others.

We have received gifts to bless others, and in doing so, we glorify the giver of these gifts. "Having gifts that differ according to the grace given to us, let us use them: if prophecy, in proportion to our faith; if service, in our serving; the one who teaches, in his teaching; the one who exhorts, in his exhortation; the one who contributes, in generosity; the one who leads, with zeal; the one who does acts of mercy, with cheerfulness." (Romans 12:6-8)

These words from Paul not only name the gifts but also the heart behind the gifts, namely giving in generosity, showing mercy with cheerfulness, and leading with zeal. The Lord never gives half-heartedly; therefore, we should never use our gifts half-heartedly in blessing others. We can compare blessings to running water – the wider we open the tap, the more water streams out.

Gifts received from the Lord are not always big, drawing front-page news. A gift could be a desire and love to bake or clean or cook. These are all ways to make the lives of those in need easier.

As members of the body of Christ, we do not all have the same function in the church. Therefore, we don't show the same gifts. To succeed, we must learn to collaborate and appreciate each other's talents. Thus, we should keep in mind the message of 1 Corinthians 12:15, which states, "If the foot should say, 'Because I am not a hand, I do not belong to the body,' that would not make it any less a part of the body."

**REFLECTION: Exodus 31:3-6  James 1: 17-18**

_____
_____
_____
_____
_____
_____
_____

# 13
# Visualise Answered Prayer

We were travelling on one of those typical straight roads on our way to the city. Four hundred kilometres of highway with hardly a bend in the road is how one could describe most roads in South Africa. The only passenger was our eight-year-old younger daughter. She was a dreamer, and I could see she was in that state of mind again.

Her question snapped me back to the present as I was lost in my thoughts: "Mum, do you ever pray for my husband? He must be born already and is somewhere on this earth."

"To be honest, I haven't ever thought about that," I admitted.

"Well, Mum, then you better ask Jesus that his parents would raise him to be a good person because then he will be a good husband, too."

Her innocent request was a powerful reminder that it is never too early to pray for something, just as it is never too late to pray for something.

An example from the Bible is the story of Hannah in 1 Samuel 1. Elkanah had two wives, Peninnah and Hannah. Elkanah loved Hannah more, but she was childless while Peninnah bore him children. Elkanah assured Hannah time and time again that he did not love her less because of her being childless. Unfortunately, she could not help feeling inferior to Peninnah, who did not let an opportunity pass without reminding Hannah of her own status as mother to Elkanah's children.

During one of their yearly visits to the temple, Hannah prayed in great distress to the Lord, asking Him to give her a son. She also vowed she would give him back to the Lord if He would only answer her prayer. Within a year, the Lord, in his faithfulness, answered her prayer. She called her son Samuel. By the time he became weaned, she handed Samuel over to Eli, the priest, for training in temple service.

The basis of prayer is faith, but visualising the answer to your prayer is to trust with all your heart. Hannah did just that. Before knowing her prayer would be answered, Hannah made a promise to the Lord that she would return her son to Him and allow him to serve the Lord. As time passed, Samuel became one of the most important prophets in the Bible.

Hannah made a sincere commitment to the Lord, even though she could not foresee the eventual outcome of that commitment. This commitment came from deep gratitude, as if the Lord had already answered her prayer. She set an example of not making promises to the Lord in our hour of need, to forget them after our prayers have been answered.

Hannah had no such intention of manipulating the Lord into answering her prayer for her own benefit. She submitted herself completely to the Lord, as we see in 1 Samuel 1:11. Her grief was genuine and her longing intense. She admitted her dependency on the Lord and craved His intervention. She acknowledged she was His servant and left to His mercy, which is a place that many of us can testify to have been at certain times in our lives. We acknowledge our total dependency on God and understand that our prayers are answered in His own good time.

Let us humble ourselves before the Lord in prayer. Humility is the basis of praise, as we see in Hannah's prayer of praise in 1 Samuel 2:1-2. She understood the difference between God and us humans, acknowledging, "There is none holy like the Lord: for there is none besides you; There is no rock like our God. Talk no more so very proudly. Let not arrogance come from your mouth; for the Lord is a God of knowledge, and by him actions are weighed."

**REFLECTION: 1 Samuel 2:1-11**

# 14
# Believe Half and Half-Not

In 1994, my husband, two teenage daughters, and myself, arrived on the West Coast of New Zealand's South Island. After settling in as new migrants, I met a lovely Christian lady who later became a lifelong friend. She taught Religious Education, or as known then, Bible in Schools. She asked if I would be interested in helping her with teaching weekly lessons at a nearby primary school. I was eager to accept and could see the Lord's hand in this request since I had always been involved in children's ministry in South Africa. I could not picture life in this unfamiliar country without experiencing the joy of working with children in some capacity again.

Accepting her invitation turned into a twenty-one-year blessing teaching Bible in Schools. I started teaching the Year Two students.

At my very first school in New Zealand, there was one boy with the brightest blue eyes. He was an intelligent little fellow who hung off my every word in our lessons. I could see the content of the lessons intrigued and fascinated him, and it was clearly his first encounter with the Bible. However, one day when I walked through the door, he was waiting for me and the first thing he said was, "I don't believe that God made animals, birds, or anything."

"And why don't you believe God made everything?"

His response to my answer: "Because my parents say we don't go to church."

I understood this was his parents' way of saying that they were not Christians, avoiding going into detail with their six-year-old son. Some months later, the class got an old computer donated, and they were very excited about this recent addition. I remarked it showed how clever God made us; He gave us minds on assembling computers and understanding how things worked.

This blue-eyed boy must have pondered this, because he met me at the door as I left, and said, "I think I believe half and half-not."

Maybe we can also look back on a time when we believed only half and half-not, or maybe even still feel like that. This did not happen overnight but could be a gradual waning of our faith. The world says 'everything goes'. It also spells out that there is no such thing as sin; it is only Christians who believe in sin. The world expects us not to defend our Christian beliefs, either. But no matter how the world tries to make sin acceptable, "If we say we have no sin, we deceive ourselves, and the truth is not in us." (1 John 1:8)

Often, this gradual decline decreases our interest or desire to read and study the Bible. Prayer seems less important. Before one knows it, the 'half-not' of faith has settled in. This is a warning that the next phase could be a full-blown case of 'believe not'.

Nowhere in the Bible is it suggested that it is possible to believe only halfway. The Christian faith is the whole truth based on the Word of God. There are many theories circulating about the authenticity of the Bible, but educated, god-fearing men and women can counteract them. Things become even more confusing when clergy selectively accept certain aspects of the Bible – for example, acknowledging that Jesus died on the cross but denying his resurrection.

It is clear in Hebrews 11:6, "And without faith it is impossible to please him, for whoever would draw near to God must believe that he exists and that he rewards those who seek him."

**REFLECTION: 2 Timothy 2:8-13**

___
___
___
___
___
___
___

# 15
# For His Own Pleasure

After two years on the West Coast, we moved to a small rural town in Otago. Here I continued teaching Bible in Schools for many years. It was during one such session with Year Five students that the lesson included a question about why God created the world.

A couple of eager hands shot up. The first student's answer was, "God was bored." Another answered, "He wanted to create a playground for us."

Was He bored? Definitely not! That is a human term and shows a lack of self-discipline. Did He want to create a playground for us? Through a child's eyes, I could see why that made sense. In the late nineties, the news wasn't solely about global tragedies. These students lived in a farming community and life was uncomplicated. They were happy and had fun in *God's playground*.

Though the answers were not lacking in originality and were even amusing, the question aimed to uncover the purpose God had in mind when He created the earth, the heavens, and every living thing.

In the story of creation as written in Genesis 1, God created the earth first to prepare for man. It was a perfect place for Adam and Eve to live and enjoy God, and in doing so they glorified Him and the works of His hands.

We read God looked at what He created day by day, and He was pleased. "And God saw everything that he had made, and behold, it was very good. And there was evening and there was morning, the sixth day." (Genesis 1:31)

Unfortunately, this perfect world God created for man became tainted through Adam and Eve's disobedience. They rebelled against God by listening to the serpent. Adam and Eve's disobedience affected not only themselves but also resulted in the whole curse of creation. Gone was the perfect beauty and harmony in nature and among man.

God, in His great love and mercy, did not remove all beauty from this earth because of the fall of Adam and Eve. Faith in Jesus as the Son of God restores beauty in our hearts. Faith allows us "to put on the new self, created after the likeness of God in true righteousness and holiness." (Ephesians 4:24)

Then there is creation itself; though cursed with storms, floods, and droughts, it is bursting with beauty. The variety in nature cannot be the work of humanity itself. Psalm 8 is a song of praise to the Lord: "When I look at your heavens, the work of your fingers, the moon and the stars which you have set in place ... all sheep and oxen and also the beasts of the field, the birds of the heavens, and the fish of the sea, whatever passes along the paths of the seas."

It is too wonderful that God entrusted his creation to man, as it says in Psalm 8:5-6, "Yet you have made him a little lower than the heavenly beings and crowned him with glory and honour. You have given him dominion over the works of your hands; you have put all things under his feet."

May we look further than a child and not see this earth as a playground to have fun and do whatever is our liking. Let us see it as granted by God to enjoy by honouring Him and all the blessings He provides through creation. We should keep in mind that it pleases Him greatly if we take care of the works of His hands – but it may please Him too if we show the same pleasure as a child on a playground, enjoying it to the full in sincerity.

May our voices harmonise with creation in a song of praise, "O Lord, our Lord, how majestic is your name in all the earth!" (Psalm 8:9)!

**REFLECTION: Psalms 104:1-25**

_____
_____
_____
_____

# 16
# A Big Yes

I started a tradition by giving my students a volume of the New Testament as a Christmas gift at the end of each school year. Most of them appreciated the gesture, but there were also those who would glance at it once and showed no further interest. But I prayed that the Holy Spirit would change those attitudes as time passed.

It was a joy to experience an immediate answer to my prayers on one such occasion. Before I handed out the New Testaments, I would tell the children that it was theirs to keep. While I was telling the class this, one student, who usually kept to himself, jumped up with a glowing face and yelled, "Yes, yes! I've always wanted a Bible! Could I please have mine first?"

There were other occasions where parents would meet me in the street or see me at a shop and thank me for the gift or say how much their child enjoyed reading the Bible. These parents were no churchgoers or even believers. Often, they had some knowledge gained from Sunday School lessons as a child, but as they grew up it had become irrelevant. I was always thankful hearing their comments. It filled me with gratitude that they did not discourage their children from reading these New Testaments.

We cannot point fingers at those who don't realise the Bible's relevance; how many of us have experienced a period in our lives where we lost the desire to read the Bible daily? Perhaps some of us were just as enthusiastic as this student when we got our first Bible, but over time we lost our appetite for it.

Maybe it was too much of an effort; we may not have had the time. Maybe worldliness took over and doubt crept into our faith, or we felt not worthy enough to reach out to the Bible. Often, a guilty conscience can withhold us from reading the Bible.

Whatever the reason, the result is always the same: progression from indifference to a dryness in spirit that often leads to deep feelings of being out of touch with the Lord. Sometimes we may think the Lord has left us, but it is the other way around; it is we who move away, not God, who never moves away. He is unmovable and unchangeable. (Hebrews 13:8)

So, if that is the case, why is it important to read and study the Scriptures? It is not a requirement of salvation, but it enriches our spirit, nurtures our faith, brings us closer to the Lord, teaches us about our own sin and, above all, it shows us the deity of God and His role in our lives. The Bible is a mirror that reflects God's tender kindness and steadfast love. It instils in us a love and adoration for who He is, and because of that, we desire to love and serve one another as Jesus loved and served.

An unread Bible is like a treasure chest standing in a room, dusty and forgotten. Upon receiving the chest, you open it, only to find its contents disappointing. With a single glance, you see nothing of value, and it means little to you. However, you do not know what you are missing out on, because if you allow yourself the time to search further, you will find another compartment with wonderful gems, and after you have explored these and think you are done, you will find another compartment containing more amazing gems. It is then that you decide to keep on searching, because discovering one gem after another is most enriching. Like a treasure hunter, you will become greedy for more of these gems.

The treasures the Bible contains are like no other. You will gain beautiful gems of wisdom, insight, and understanding, as well as knowledge by reading the Bible.

**REFLECTION: Proverbs 2:1-11**

# 17
# Faith Like a Marshmallow

Any teacher would agree that children learn much better when they take active part in a lesson. In one of my Bible in Schools classes, the story of the day was about David and Goliath. The students were quiet as mice as the story unfolded. When I got to the part of David challenging Goliath, the tension in the room was palpable.

Eager eleven-year-old hands went up when I asked who wanted to show how David killed Goliath. I chose a quiet boy and handed him a marshmallow 'stone' and handkerchief with knots at the end, representing the slingshot. These 'weapons' were the safest in a classroom setting.

Earlier, I had put a poster of Goliath on the whiteboard. Aiming, the student's shot fell short of the target because of its marshmallow-like softness. Although the children enjoyed the action, 'David' especially found it amusing. In the week that followed, I asked the students if they remembered who killed Goliath. The chosen student of the previous week jumped up and said, "I did, I did!" I am sure even David himself would have found that funny, too.

How often do we as adults try to kill the Goliaths in our lives with faith as squishy and without substance as that of a marshmallow? No wonder those Goliaths remain immovable. If David's faith lacked substance, he would not have challenged Goliath. So, what made his faith so strong that he, with full conviction, stepped out and challenged the most feared enemy of that time?

The answer did not lie in an impulsive act but started long before the day he faced Goliath. David realised the power of God when he protected his sheep against the wild beasts of the field. He was a young, ordinary boy but relied on the strength of the Lord to protect the flock his father entrusted him to shepherd. He experienced in the solitude of nature an awareness of the Lord's presence. The Psalms of David are full of phrases about meditation on the various attributes of the Lord.

When David faced Goliath, he said, "The Lord who delivered me from the paw of the lion and from the paw of the bear will deliver me from the hand of this Philistine." These words to Goliath were a testimony to David's knowledge of who God was (1 Samuel 17: 37).

David had a close relationship with the Lord. The words in 1 Samuel 13:14 suggests that: "The Lord has sought for Himself a man after His own heart."

This relationship between the Lord and David flowed from the faith David had in the all-powerful God. David did not see himself as a young man with no training in warfare. He forgot who he was and kept his eyes focused on his God, trusting Him with his life. Unwavering, he stepped out in faith, knowing his courage and strength rested in God, which made him fearless in the face of his enemy.

How many of us have faced Goliaths in our own lives? Are we building a strong faith through a close relationship with the Lord, so that in those days in which we will need courage, strength in spirit, and fearlessness, we could stand firm? Meditating on the Word, soaking ourselves in it and communicating with the Lord through prayer is essential to grow in faith. It is only then that we can face the enemy with courage and an unwavering faith regardless of the enormity of a testing time. "If you are not firm in faith, you are not firm at all." (Isaiah 7:9)

**REFLECTION: Romans 5:1-11**

_____
_____
_____
_____
_____
_____
_____

# 18
# It is My Life

It was a one-off favour when I offered to mind a nine-year-old one afternoon while his mother was out. He was bright, observant, and had a unique view of nature. He once shared with me his dismay of being told off by a teacher when he climbed a pine tree that grew on the school grounds.

"I enjoy climbing trees. Trees that bear no fruit have no function except to be climbed."

It was hard not to smile at this observation. Who could find fault with such reasoning?

On this specific afternoon, our conversation was not about trees, but about the previous weekend he spent with his grandparents. He had a lot to share, especially about going with them to church. His parents were not believers, and the church played no role in their lives. Apparently, that was not the case with his grandparents. Halfway through his account of attending church, he became very serious and said, "The pastor said we must give our lives to Jesus. But why should I give my life away? It is my life."

Aren't we all born with this belief, which, as we get older, grows into a sense of rebellion against a higher authority? Children are never too young to show this rebellion. Even before they can verbalise it in words, their actions spell it out: "It is *my* life, therefore I can have *my* way. Don't tell me what to do. I am in charge."

Adam and Eve were the first humans to rebel against God and his command when He told them, "You may surely eat of every tree of the garden, but of the tree of the knowledge of good and evil you shall not eat, for in the day that you eat of it you shall surely die." (Genesis 2:16-17) By listening to the serpent and going against the command of God, Adam and Eve set the whole human race on a path of rebellion, fed by sin.

The word sin is only a three-letter word, but in the lower case the *i* became a capital letter *I* the moment Adam and Eve tasted the forbidden fruit. It became all about me. Throughout the centuries, that has remained unchanged. If rulers want their way and they fail, they start wars which lead to destruction and death. If individuals cannot have their way, they war against each other, causing hurt and pain, leaving relationships in tatters.

There is also a war within to reckon with. The war of discontentment, caused by our own self-centredness, which makes us to believe we deserve happiness, peace, fulfilment, riches, and fairness. We have an attitude that says, "It is my right to live my life as I please…"

Each of us is born with a spiritual, leaky heart. We can only close the valve and plug the leak when we allow Jesus to seal it with His cross. When we realise the folly of our rebellion and invite Him to take over, a miracle happens. Instead of losing everything, we gain everything that we always wanted. Happiness, fulfilment, peace, and riches far greater than this world can offer.

It only takes one step, a willingness to believe in Jesus as our Saviour, for the gates of abundance to be opened. When it is not about us anymore but about Jesus, it is then that the following becomes visible in our lives, and we become able to follow and love Him.

"Now to him who is able to do far more abundantly than all that we ask or think, according to the power at work within us, to him be glory in the church and in Christ Jesus throughout all generations, forever and ever." (Ephesians 3:20-21)

**REFLECTION: Galatians 5:16-26**

___
___
___
___
___
___
___

# 19
# Unconditional Love

As I entered the classroom one cold morning, it surprised me to see the teacher in the process of addressing my Bible in School's class. The custom was usually that she busied herself while the students sat quietly, waiting for my arrival. By the sound of it, she was very serious.

When she noticed me, she said to the students, "And what do you think Mrs Dittrich will think of you when she hears about the bullying that goes on in this class?"

Before she could utter another word, one boy jumped up and said, "She loves us and prays for us every day. She said it herself."

The surprised teacher had no comment after that and handed the class over to me.

This incident reminded me of how important it is to others, knowing that you are praying for them. Also, the message that prayer and love go together. These children came from a range of backgrounds. Although most of them were not raised with Christian teachings by their parents, they understood that there was an unseen God who could be trusted. They were also beginning to realise that they were important to me and that I valued them. However, they did not realise that this stemmed from my love for the Lord, a fact I hoped they would grasp as the year went on.

It filled me with joy, realising this boy's remark came from the assurance that there was no judgement from me. My affection, or love, as he observed, was unconditional.

But are we not loved by the Lord Jesus unconditionally? He is the perfect example of unconditional love. "God shows his love for us in that while we were still sinners, Christ died for us." (Romans 5:8) From the beginning of time, no sin has ever been so big that Jesus could not pay its penalty on the cross.

There is also nothing we can do to receive his love. No good works, piety, a pure life, or any kind of effort from our side can earn his love or pay for what He suffered on the cross on our behalf.

If Jesus could do this for us because of His love, how can we ever withhold our love from one another? "Beloved, let us love one another, for love is from God, and whoever loves has been born of God and knows God." (1 John 4:7)

For us to love, we must know God. That knowledge leads to understanding who He is – an understanding that He is love, therefore His love is unchangeable, everlasting, and immeasurable. This understanding paves the way not only to loving God, but to loving one another.

The Scripture states that when we love our brothers and sisters and see they are in need, we should help them if we have the world's goods to do so (1 John 3:16). We have access to an abundance of spiritual goods, as in prayer. We can feed and dress countless others with the spiritual abundance our prayers provide.

Taking hold of the love of God, accepting it, and making it our own, will cause the banks of our hearts to overflow in love for one another. A love that will lead to an unstoppable desire to serve and pray for one another.

When Jesus was led to the cross, He did not consider the cost. Let us also not calculate the cost of our love in giving, serving, and praying for one another.

"Little children, let us not love in word or talk but in deed and in truth." (1 John 3:18)

## REFLECTION: John 13:12-20

_____
_____
_____
_____
_____
_____
_____

# 20
# Make Peace With

My five-year-old granddaughter was helping me dust the bookshelves when she noticed a bright yellow book amongst the others. Curiously, she wanted to know what the book was about. Like all children, she loved stories and thought I could read this book to her on the spot. With her being the first grandchild and doted on, everything came to a standstill when she wanted a story to be read.

I explained it was a book for adults. Having an inquisitive mind, she wanted me to tell her the title, seeing that the title was in Afrikaans.

Upon hearing that the title translated as *Make Peace With*, she responded by saying, "Your parents should've read that book – maybe it would've prevented their divorce."

I was at a loss for words. I could not believe that she had associated the absence of peace with my parents' divorce, something I had shared with her a couple of days prior when she had wanted to know why her great grandparents were no longer together.

Sadly, a lack of peace from within ourselves will affect the people closest to us.

We all strive to have peace and to live peaceful lives. However, if we decide to maintain inner peace and live peaceful lives by doing it in our own strength, we could expect to fail time and time again. As sinful beings, we carry the seeds of discontentment, self-righteousness, egotism, entitlement, and selfishness within our hearts. These are all enemies of peace. Peace does not come naturally. It competes with the self-centredness which rules our hearts and minds. Non-Christians are not the only ones who struggle with a lack of peace. Many Christians have a lifelong struggle to find inner peace.

Jesus knows us better than we can ever know ourselves. It is not only our sin, but fear that prevents an ever-present peace – fear of the unknown that awaits us, the state of the world, fear of failure, even fear about our own safety and that of our loved ones. There is a never-ending list of fears that steal our peace. But Jesus reassures us in John 14:27, "Peace I leave with you; my peace I give to you. Not as the world gives do I give to you. Let not your hearts be troubled, neither let them be afraid."

So, what makes the peace of Jesus so different from the peace of the world? The world portrays peace as being happy, and to be happy, you must have things, be successful, and have perfect relationships. According to the world, these things not only make you happy, but you will have peace and be able to live a peaceful life.

As we go through life, we may see glimpses of peace in the world and in the lives of others. But sadly, it never lasts. It is a yo-yo peace.

When we believe in Jesus' death on the cross and accept that He is the Son of God, we have become righteous before Him: "And the effect of righteousness will be peace, and the result of righteousness, quietness and trust forever." (Isaiah 32:17)

It is amazing how we can all experience real, everlasting peace, made possible through faith in Jesus Christ. Through faith, we receive the Holy Spirit, who blesses us with fruits of the Spirit, (Galatians 5:22). One of these fruits is peace, a peace that settles within and overflows to others. This peace transcends all understanding. It is available to all who believe in Jesus, love Him, desire a close relationship with Him, and live in the wonderful knowledge of being cleansed and forgiven. This relationship enables us to become a channel of peace in a peaceless world. "And he said, 'O man greatly loved fear not, peace be with you.'" (Daniel 10:19)

**REFLECTION: Philippians 4:4-9**

# 21
# The Good Soil

One bitter chilly morning, being wrapped up for the weather down south, a student's unexpected remark warmed my heart. She came up to me and said quietly, "Mrs Dittrich, I hope my heart will be good soil for the seed."

She was, of course, referring to the Parable of The Sower (Matthew 13:1-9, 18-23). The students listened well that morning to this parable, some more intently than others, as was usually the case in a classroom full of students.

That was also the experience of Jesus as the greatest teacher of all time. During the telling of this parable, He referred to what the prophet Isaiah said, "You will be ever hearing but never understanding; you will be ever seeing but never perceiving."

But on this day, there was at least one student who heard and perceived and therefore desired for her heart to be good soil. Praise the Lord for that.

It may seem like a mystery how some hearts become good soil and others not. According to Jesus' explanation, the latter happens when there is a lack of understanding, a shallowness of heart, or over-riddled with thorns as cares of this world. But we must be careful not to deceive ourselves, thinking that our hearts are good soil while being blind to notice the parts that do not allow the seed to take root.

Jesus used this parable effectively. A sower could be a farmer or anyone who sows seeds with the goal of reaping abundantly. He chooses the best soil where it gets the warmth of the sun. Then he weeds the chosen soil to get rid of all unwanted growths. He may add some nutrients to the soil as nourishment and to improve the fermentation. The soil is prepared to receive the seed at this stage. He waters it faithfully. He protects the young seedlings with netting against birds and the elements.

Considering the above, we know Jesus is the Sower. He looks at our hearts and sees its potential to become good soil. A potential that originates from a desire, a hunger, a thirst to receive the seed, which is the Word. Preparation of our hearts often starts unknowingly much earlier because He first loved us. He makes us aware of our need for Him, but with that, we become deeply aware of the weeds (sin). He will gladly remove it if we accept His forgiveness. Our hearts are prepared by being nourished by the work of the Holy Spirit, and the Sower sows the Word. We receive all the spiritual nutrients we need. That includes understanding, trust, and grasping the effect of the cares of this world. His protection is the net of knowledge which leads to the fear of the Lord and, ultimately, wisdom.

Seeds need water, and the sun to sprout and grow to become the plants they are. This is most needed to produce the fruit expected, and so it is with our hearts as good soil. We need Jesus as the Son of God. He is also the Light in this dark world and is the living water to all those hearts who receive the Word and understand it. He indeed bears fruit and yields, in one case a hundredfold, in another sixty, and in another thirty.

May we hear with great gratitude the voice of Jesus saying, "But blessed are your eyes, for they see, and your ears, for they hear. For truly, I say to you, many prophets and righteous people longed to see what you see, and not see it, and to hear what you hear, and did not hear it." (Matthew 13:16-17)

**REFLECTION: Matthew 13:24-30       Matthew 13:36-43**

# 22
# Imprisonment

I shared a true story with the students, who listened eagerly. I had their full attention. They were really interested to see where this story was going.

It was about a prisoner who received a Bible from a Christian pastoral group. This prisoner was a heavy smoker and every time he ran out of cigarettes, he would use tobacco and a page of the Bible to roll his own cigarette. After some time, he ran out of Bible pages, none of which he had read. One morning he was desperate for a smoke. He had the tobacco, but no pages left. He bent down to look under his bed, thinking there might just be a piece he missed. To his joy, he noticed this small piece of paper, the last of his Bible. He grabbed it, but just before he started covering his tobacco with it, he felt compelled to read the words.

It was John 3:16, "For God so loved the world, that he gave his only Son, that whoever believes in him should not perish but have eternal life."

A loud exclamation of a student interrupted the class's concentration.

"Wow! He must have smoked a lot because there are hundreds of pages in the Bible."

Though the remark was quite amusing, I lost my concentration for a moment. I reminded the class that this is not about this man's smoking habit, but about God's power.

The power of God's word changes people, no matter where they are or their circumstances. John 3:16 deeply touched the prisoner, and he realised he needed to believe in Jesus as the Son of God. If God so loved the world to give His own Son, then he had to be included in such a love. He requested a new Bible, not for smoking but to familiarise himself with the contents. He started reading for hours on end. Within days, he experienced a new freedom, a freedom he never could imagine existed before. Despite being confined to the four walls of a cell, he experienced a sense of freedom in his heart. This prisoner discovered the truth of Jesus' words, "If you abide in my word, you are truly my disciples, and you will know the truth, and the truth will set you free." (John 8:31)

The power the Bible has in people's lives brings lasting renewal. The prisoner experienced renewal that could only take place through the working of the Holy Spirit. Jesus explains in John 3:3, "Truly, truly, I say to you, unless one is born again, he cannot see the kingdom of God."

Though few of us can say we know the inside of a cell, we are all imprisoned by sin or as Jesus describes it, "…everyone who practices sin is a slave to sin." (John 8:34)

Often, we as believers feel good about ourselves because we have faith. We attend church and Bible study groups, and visit the sick and frail regularly. We look at our lives and it is in such a contrast to the surrounding secular world. The temptation is to forget that we are sinners too.

Sadly, some of us have never experienced the wonder of being born again. Lacking experience of renewal results from not abiding in the Word. If that is the case, we become imprisoned, or rather enslaved by allowing the world to influence our way of thinking and acting, and by compromising. This eventually leads us away from the Lord and his Word.

In Romans 6:16 there is the following warning, "Do you not know that if you present yourselves to anyone as obedient slaves, you are slaves of the one whom you obey, either of sin, which leads to death, or of obedience, which leads to righteousness?"

**REFLECTION: John 3:1-21**

## 23
## What If?

This cute little girl was only four years old when she entered our lives. I was chaplain at the local area school and liaison between parents and the school. Her dad was a solo parent and with the mum out of the picture, they needed help.

We became surrogate grandparents and found great joy in having her once a week and later during the school holidays.

During one of these school holidays when she was nine or ten, at bedtime she made a remark that was quite astonishing. As usual, we read the Bible together and prayed before we said goodnight.

She said, "I am glad Adam and Eve ate from the forbidden tree."

Quite shocked, I asked why she felt that way. Without hesitation, she answered, "Just think how many people would be on this earth if nobody ever died. It would be so claustrophobic."

What could I say? Never had I heard that view before. Her remark surprised me, but I did not argue. I remarked I did not know how life would have been without disobedience. We can be very thankful that God had a plan for this world knowing Adam and Eve were going to disobey. His plan was to send Jesus to cancel out their disobedience, by being Himself obedient to the Father, even to death. Being in late primary, she understood well.

I'm sure many believers wondered throughout the centuries about some biblical accounts, leading to many of the 'what if' questions. But instead of wondering about the implications of an unfallen Adam and Eve, let us rather think about the *good* that came from it.

It must have been a huge grieving experience for Adam and Eve to lose all their wonderful privileges. Being surrounded by God's continual presence allowed them to experience privileges that must have been amazing. But thankfully it didn't end there. God was prepared to redeem humankind and to restore the relationship with Him through Jesus Christ's death and resurrection.

We still carry the consequences of their sin by being just as sinful. But this doesn't mean the suffering caused through them by sinning against God aims solely to cause heartache for humankind. No, the risen Jesus and the example of His perfect godliness, as illustrated in the Bible, cancelled out the huge negative impact of the fall of Adam and Eve.

Sin became an instrument in God's hand to teach us step-by-step that, like in the Garden of Eden, His presence is still with us. We experience that wherever pain is, there is also His abounding grace. Wherever there is judgement, there is forgiveness. Where there is fear, there is the assurance of protection (2 Timothy 4:18). We receive strength accordingly in our daily struggles, whether they are big or small. Whatever the need, provision is at hand. When there is grief, comfort comes (Isaiah 61:3). Whenever there is a pressure of any kind, He lifts us up with wings like eagles (Isaiah 40:31).

We can long for a perfect world, but in this broken, sinful world we learn to be thankful to our Creator and to give Him all the honour and glory. Humanity has not forever lost the perfect world that Adam and Eve initially experienced. We can look forward with hope to be eternally with God in time to come.

Through Jesus, He made us more than conquerors and promised in Revelation 3:21, "The one who conquers, I will grant him to sit with me on my throne, as I also conquered and sat down with my Father on his throne."

**REFLECTION: Psalm 103**

# 24
# A Blend of Life and Faith

My granddaughter, then in her early teens, and I had a conversation about heaven. She shared her view of how she thought it would look there. She always had a vivid imagination and painted heaven appropriately with descriptive words. When she finished, she added, "And you, Ouma [Afrikaans for grandma], will live in a mansion while most of us will only be in tents."

Surprised, I asked why she thought that would be the case.

"For you, life and faith blend, but for most of us, faith is on one side while life is on the other. Therefore, you will get a mansion in heaven."

Most commentators have agreed over decades that Jesus did not mean that heaven will have different places for us to live in, but that there will be enough room in heaven for all believers. Translators replaced the word 'mansion' (which means a room in Hebrew) with the word 'room' in later translations. "Jesus said, in my Father's house are many rooms." (John 14:2) Jesus wanted His disciples to know that there will be enough space for every believer to worship God together in heaven and to share equally the presence of God with no assigned dwellings.

I explained this to my dear granddaughter, but she did not want to accept that. To her mind, there would be different dwellings. I just left it there and decided it is not good to argue about minor details with a young teenager.

Her observation made me realise the huge responsibility believers have in the way we express our faith in everyday life. Also, the impression it leaves on those who are close to us, as well as on those whoever crosses our path.

Relatives, friends, and others who are aware we are Christians are watching our daily walk closely. Mostly, they are not even doing it consciously. There will be those who find encouragement in the example we set in being disciplined and dedicated in our worship and fellowship meeting with other. The joy they notice we find in caring and helping others should be encouraging.

Then there are those who are the closest. Our family who spends most of the time with us. They are watching, too. Our involvements with Christian activities and our compassion for whoever is struggling around us, may only be part of the image we like to portray to the world. For when at home, the joy, patience, tolerance, caring, understanding and love may be lacking. Do they notice any personal time being set aside for prayer and Bible reading amid our Christian activities? Maybe they observe we treat family devotions as a chore, hastily being fitted in once a day.

Some of us may give the impression that being a follower of Christ consists only of church attendance and involvement with Christian activities. For the rest, it is business as usual, with no difference between the believer and non-believer in the way daily life is being taken care of – confirming clearly that faith and daily life are two separate entities.

But is that God's way? Our commitment to the church, caring and helping inside and outside the church, must express our love and devotion to Christ. If that is the case, then faith and life blend. Faith without being incorporated into our daily lives moment by moment is a diluted faith. No, let us rather be "watchful, stand firm in the faith, act like men [women], be strong. Let all you do be done in love." (1 Corinthians 16:13-14)

**REFLECTION: 1 Corinthians 13**

_____
_____
_____
_____
_____
_____
_____

# 25
# Be Yourself

In the early 2000s, I became a facilitator of various programmes aimed at children who needed help to cope with traumatic situations. One of these programmes was to help children with behavioural problems.

One morning during a session with an eleven-year-old boy, he interrupted me abruptly and said, "Mrs Dittrich, you know how I sit right at the front close to the teacher, because I am a problem? Well, yesterday morning after the Bible in Schools lesson when you left, I overheard a remark coming from my teacher to another teacher about you being such a Christian, a real goodie-good, and how it irritates her."

Without realising, I uttered my thoughts aloud, more to myself, "I wonder how to act from here onwards."

His reply followed immediately and took me completely by surprise.

"Do nothing. Just continue to be yourself."

Well, coming from a boy with extreme destructive behaviour, he blew me away. If it was allowable, I would have given him a big hug.

His remark made me realise that the judgemental, critical staff member worsened his behaviour by failing to show empathy. The complexity of his situation was extreme. His father was absent from his life, his mother had an addiction problem, and his brother was in prison. Still, he knew right from wrong, and what he overheard was not right and not acceptable. But he realised it was not worth it to do anything. He knew the hardness of a heart when he saw it. He had been exposed to that since birth.

This incident was a powerful reminder of the world Jesus entered. The judgemental, critical religious leaders who thought they were the only authority in knowledge of the law challenged Jesus. Even ordinary people were more interested in what Christ could do than in who he really was. The Jews wanted a Messiah that could destroy their enemies, not a suffering Messiah as described in Isaiah 53 and Psalm 22.

Even Jesus' brothers did not believe in Him. In John 7:3-5, they challenge Him by saying to Jesus that He should go to Judea where the feast of Booths was going to take place. "For no one works in secret if he seeks to be known openly. If you do these things, show yourself to the world."

Jesus is the perfect example to all his followers. In his role as the Son of God, he persisted in being Himself in who He was. He never tried to live up to the people's expectations or tried to please them. He came to this earth to obey His Father's will and to pay the highest price on the cross. But during His three-year ministry followed by his death, He brought not only healing to those who suffered physically, but also healing of the heart by showing and teaching people the truth. This is continuing throughout His word.

In following Jesus, do we really expect that it will be a straightforward journey? If we desire to be liked, accepted, and to impress all people with what we do and believe, then we are deceiving ourselves. Believers must be ready not to meet the world's standards of popularity. "Be not surprised brothers, that the world hates you." (1 John 3:13)

Rather, let us pray for those who criticise, dislike, or even persecute us. In Luke 6:35 the command is, "But love your enemies and do good and lend, expecting nothing in return, and your reward will be great, and you will be sons of the Most High, for he is kind to the ungrateful and the evil. Be merciful, even as your Father is merciful." (Luke 6:35-36)

**REFLECTION: Luke 6:37-42**

## 26
## The Devil is Gone, But…

During the mid-1970s, I was the sole breadwinner while my husband was busy completing his medical studies. Therefore, our son was attending a kindergarten, and it made me felt quite guilty whenever I needed someone to child-mind him the odd time it was outside hours.

One afternoon I had to attend a doctor's appointment, and arranged with a neighbour for her nanny to take care of our son.

When I went to pick up my four-year-old, I walked in on a scene where he was yelling at the nanny. He was brushing off something invisible on his one shoulder.

Angrily he yelled, "The devil is gone but I still don't like you!"

He probably picked up the expression 'the devil on your shoulder' at the kindergarten. I was quite embarrassed and demanded that he apologise to the nanny, which he did reluctantly.

From the nanny's perspective, she probably thought, "The devil may be gone, but you are still a naughty boy."

There are many kinds of *devils on shoulders in this world*, either caused by others to you or the other way round. So many are suffering as the result of bad choices, bad influences, circumstances, and abuse of various kinds. Everyone is vulnerable to these things since birth. Maybe you have become the 'devil on the shoulder' of another by making them suffer because you are hurting.

The testimonies of others who have overcome and brushed the devil off their shoulders never fail to amaze us. Some of us, though, wonder how long that will last when the testimony is all about how they healed themselves in their own strength. Sadly, many who overcame and turned their lives around with the intervention of other professionals, eventually turn back to their old ways.

So, what is the cure to remove *the devil from your shoulder* and become a new person permanently? The answer lies in one Person, Jesus Christ, whose grace is abounding.

We can look at Jesus, and see and experience the grace that pours from Him. His grace extends beyond the victim. The same grace covers the one who caused the harm. The reason is that we are all sinners, "But God shows his love for us in that while we were still sinners, Christ died for us." (Romans 5:8)

A good example is the Samaritan woman at the well (John 4:7-45). When she brought water for Jesus to drink at his request, He used the opportunity to tell her He is the living water. She realised He knew about her adultery, but He showed her grace – not condemning her, rather telling her not to sin anymore. She returned to the town and many Samaritans believed in Him because of the woman's testimony, "He told me all that I ever did." (John 4:39)

The town's people who believed her and went to see and hear Jesus for themselves must have included some families who experienced her as the *devil on their shoulder* as the result of her adultery. However, they believed the woman's testimony. The same grace Jesus showed her saved them on both sides that day.

We are all sinners who received unlimited grace. We can find great comfort in the words of Jesus in 2 Corinthians 12:9, "My grace is sufficient for you, for my power is made perfect in weakness."

**REFLECTION: 2 Peter 1:11**

_____
_____
_____
_____
_____
_____
_____

# 27
# God the Creator

I clearly remembered the surprise on the Year Five students' faces when they heard about evolution. Especially the claim that we developed from apes.

"What!" exclaimed one boy. "If that is true, why are there still apes around?" A very good observation indeed.

Non-Christian scientists may have so-called proof of evolution, but they are usually atheists or agnostics. They do not believe in the existence of God. Therefore, they do not accept that He is the Creator of heaven and earth and all living things. Unbelief prevents them from reading the Bible and in discovering that all things had their beginning in God. The very first book and verse, Genesis 1:1, declares, "In the beginning, God created the heavens and the earth." Isaiah 40:28 confirms, "Have you not known? Have you not heard? The Lord is the everlasting God, the Creator of the ends of the earth."

'Nothing comes from nothing' is a well-known phrase from a song in the musical, *Sound of Music*. But the Bible differs by teaching that God as Creator created beauty out of nothing. All artists are creators, but they need tools to help them with the art they fancy. They cannot create something from nothing. That is not the case with God. Genesis 1:2 continues, "The earth was without form and void, and darkness was over the face of the deep."

The rest of the creation story is about how God spoke different aspects of creation into existence. As the All-Powerful, He can in His sovereign authority command, and it will happen.

How privileged are we to know Him as our Creator! Our souls should praise God with the Psalmist because He wonderfully made us, as stated in the verse, "For you formed my inward parts; you knitted me together in my mother's womb. I praise you, for I am fearfully and wonderfully made. Wonderful are your works; my soul knows it very well. My frame was not hidden from you, when I was being made in secret, intricately woven in the depths of the earth." (Psalm 139:13-15)

We are the only works of His hand that are made in His image. It is amazing to think that He made us in His likeness. "God said, "Let us make man in our image, after our likeness." (Genesis 1:26) He even gave us authority over everything He made (Psalm 8:6-8). That means that we are enabled to have dominion over His creation, and also to reflect and imitate Him mentally, morally, and socially.

It is foolishness to support any theory other than the Biblical truth of how all living things came into existence. Evolutionists need a lot of faith in what they believe about creation and need much more proof to justify their belief. Whereas Christians accept in a simpler faith creation as it is, because we believe in an amazing Creator, the big "I Am".

Jesus, as the Word, was with God when the world was created. "He was in the beginning with God." (John 1:2) But then the Word (Jesus) became flesh when He was born into this world. He continues to be the Creator by creating spiritually new hearts, making it possible for everyone who believes in Him to become a new creation in Him.

Maybe it is good to ask yourself where you stand in your view of creation and your place in it. Are you amazed by how wonderfully you are made? Does the wonder of that knowledge fill you with a desire to ask to become a new creation in Christ, if you have not yet?

2 Corinthians 5:17 describes the new creation, stating that if anyone is in Christ, they become a new creation. "The old has passed away; behold, the new has come."

**REFLECTION: Psalm 8     John 1:1-5**

_____
_____
_____
_____
_____
_____

# 28
# God Listens

During a visit of our 'adopted granddaughter', as she refers to herself, tears were flowing, tears of disappointment. She prayed about a serious matter for weeks, but with no answer to her prayer.

While I was trying to console her, she said between the sobs, "I guess God only listens to prayers He wants to answer."

That is not true, as the Bible teaches. But why does it often seem that some of our prayers are in vain and not answered at all?

Praying is the most efficient way to communicate with the Lord. Though it may seem to be only a one-way conversation, the Lord always listens and promises that we will receive whatever we ask according to His will. We should find great comfort in the promise in 1 John 5:14, "And this is the confidence that we have toward him, that if we ask anything according to his will he hears us."

There is always the time factor. We want an answer as soon as possible and get anxious when the answer seems to be delayed or never coming. But there are never unanswered prayers. The Lord's timing is always perfect. One thing is for sure, He is never in a hurry but He's always on time. Even His silence can be for our own good. He always knows what is best for us and often not what we think the best answer would be. Our will is never the determined factor with Him in answering our prayers. It is one of the most important aspects of prayer, as Jesus pointed out in the Lord's prayer, "Your [God's] will be done on earth as it is in heaven." (Matthew 6:10)

We should not lose heart when there is a delay in receiving an answer to a prayer. It must not stop us from being persistent in praying about a matter. Jesus used a parable of a widow who kept going to a judge, asking him to give her justice against her adversary. The judge refused, but she kept on coming back. In the end he gave her what she asked because he got weary of her continual coming back and asking. Jesus concluded, "Hear what the unrighteous judge says. And will not God give justice to his elect, who cry to him day and night?" (Luke 18:7)

The Bible states clearly that our prayer life must be based on faith. We can't ask anything in prayer while we are doubting. James wrote in chapter 1:5-6, "If any of you lack wisdom, let him ask God, who gives generously to all without reproach, and it will be given him. But let him ask in faith, with no doubting."

Also, our motives must be pure. "You ask and do not receive, because you ask wrongly, to spend it on your passions." (James 4:3)

Another important aspect of prayer is to live out the righteousness we have received in Christ. "If I had cherished iniquity in my heart, the Lord would not have listened. But truly, God has listened; he has attended to the voice of my prayer." (Psalm 66:18-19)

So no, God does not choose the prayers He views worth answering, but He chooses the best answers to the prayers we bring before His throne.

God, being sovereign, puts no limitations on when He answers our prayers. I am sure many of us experienced answers to prayers that astonished us in its abundance, much more than we asked for – not always regarding material things, but especially spiritual blessings.

There is this wonderful promise in Romans 8:32, "He who did not spare his own Son but gave him up for us all, how will he not also with him graciously give us all things."

**REFLECTION: James 5:13-18**

_____
_____
_____
_____
_____
_____

# 29
# Jesus is Light

One of our granddaughters lives with her parents overseas. Sadly, we don't see them often. She is a lovely, artistic girl and a deep thinker. On her first visit to New Zealand as a young teenager, she and I had good one-on-one times together. We talked about different topics that interested her. During one such talk, she asked me to explain to her what it means that 'Jesus is Light'. She added, "I heard Jesus is light, but I do not know what it means. I believe in angels, but that's about all. You see, I am still finding my way."

I explained to her that because of God's love for us, He opened a door with Jesus' death and resurrection. When we invite Jesus into our hearts, we receive Him as light into our lives. Jesus himself said, "I am the light of the world. Whoever follows me will not walk in darkness but will have the light of life." (John 8:12)

Jesus as Light shows us the way. Looking back, many of us can admit that there was a time that we lost our way or maybe never knew from the start there was another way, a better way than our own. Even not being aware of how lost we were before we found Jesus, or rather before He found us. His light illuminates the darkness we are all born into by inheriting our sinful nature. In His light, we see our desperate need for Him. This revelation leads to turning to Him by the power of the Holy Spirit.

When turning to Jesus, the Spirit gives us a desire to continue living in His light. That desire should lead to being faithful to Him, filling us with His Word. David wrote in Psalm 119:105, "Your word is a lamp to my feet and a light to my path." By neglecting the Word, the light will get dimmer in our hearts and the path to follow Jesus will get less visible.

With Jesus being the Light, the Spirit empowers us to reflect His light on the world. We can't hide the light when we become followers of Christ. Matthew 5:14 confirms, "You are the light of the world. A city set on a hill cannot be hidden." Our works are a further reflection of the light of Jesus. "In the same way, let your light shine before others, so that they may see your good works and give glory to your father who is in heaven." (Matthew 5:16)

But it is not only our works that reflect Jesus as Light. We have a command to share the light of the gospel with others. Reaching out to others so that they may find Jesus as the way, the truth, and the life (John 14:6). The light the gospel provides penetrates hardened hearts and brings the softness that only a newfound faith can bring. The Psalmist put it so well, "For you are the fountain of life; in your light do we see light." (Psalm 36:9)

Through the gift of faith, we receive the light of Jesus, and then we pass on the light to others through our works, conduct, and sharing of the gospel. It remains an amazing privilege to be a shining light for the Lord in this dark world.

May it be our prayer for all who are trying to find their way and are longing to find meaning in this world, that they will find Jesus as the Light. May they be able to reach a spiritual place where they can say with the Psalmist, "The Lord is my light and my salvation." (Psalm 27:1)

**REFLECTION: John 1:6-18**

_____
_____
_____
_____
_____
_____

# 30
# Hiding from God

It is hard to recall the topic of that specific Bible in Schools lesson, but I clearly remember the question I asked and the response of an eleven-year-old student.

The question was, how did they feel knowing that God was everywhere and that nothing could escape his eyes? This student was the first to put up his hand and his reply was, "I don't like it at all, because it means I can't do anything in secret."

This reminded me of a mother who shared about her pre-schooler when she told him they were going on holiday. He immediately wanted to know if Jesus was going with them, because it would be no fun if He did.

We may smile about this, but sometimes we feel like hiding from the Lord. Times when we don't feel comfortable, knowing that nothing escapes his eye.

One reason is that it is hard to own up when we make a mess of things. An excellent example was Adam and Eve, who saw firsthand how great God was, yet they fell into temptation and listened to the serpent. They thought they could hide from God after they disregarded his command. Adam blamed Eve, and Eve blamed the serpent (Genesis 3:12-13). They literally hid from God, hoping that He wouldn't find them in their nakedness. Their action paved the way for humans trying to hide their sin from God from generation to generation.

The Bible describes biblical characters hiding from God in various ways that we can relate to.

It can be by deceiving ourselves, as Jonah did when God called him to Nineveh. He was supposed to warn the city against destruction if they didn't turn to God (Jonah 1). Jonah thought, like so many of us do, that if we follow our own plans, the Lord will leave us alone and won't pursue the plans He has for us.

Underlying fear may compel us to hide from God. Like Jonah, we might fear what awaits us if we follow the Lord's plan for us. This may apply to a decision that needs to be made which will affect our future significantly. It may even expose us to physical danger, as in Jonah's case. Aware of the wickedness of the city of Nineveh, he was, however, called there by God. And so, despite going in the totally opposite direction to get as far away from God as possible, the Lord, through the storm on the sea and being in the fish's belly, turned him so that he went to Nineveh (Jonah 1–4).

The opposite of hiding from God is to move closer to Him. The Bible weaves the assurance of His love throughout its pages like a golden thread. Knowing that God loves us, and we can trust His plans for us, will drive out all fear. We will feel no need to flee from Him and hide. "There is no fear in love, but perfect love casts out fear. For fear has to do with punishment, and whoever fears has not been perfected in love." (1 John 4:18)

Another aspect that will remove any desire to hide from God is to read His love letter to us, the Bible. By studying it, meditating on it, praying over it, and absorbing the contents day by day is the best antidote to fleeing or hiding from God.

The Word will teach us a different fear. This is not a fear that will make you want to hide or even flee, but this is a fear that comes with understanding and that leads to wisdom. "The fear of the Lord is the beginning of wisdom, and the knowledge of the Holy One is insight." (Proverbs 9:10)

**REFLECTION: Proverbs 2:1-12**

_____
_____
_____
_____
_____
_____

# 31
# Good People

I suddenly felt little arms hugging me from the back. I heard my son's voice saying, "Mummy, I love Jesus with all my heart because He made you and Pappa so good."

It filled me with great joy – for two reasons. Firstly, that he loves Jesus, and secondly, that he acknowledged the role of Jesus in our lives.

I realised that caring, loving parents who made him feel safe and nurtured, make us, in his eyes, good people. He also showed an insight that these must be the attributes of Jesus, and seeing that we are followers of Jesus who is mightier than us, it is He who made us that way.

My son was too young at the time for me to explain to him that there are different reasons for goodness. There are the world's reasons and there are God's reasons.

To describe good people, we could think along the following lines: they are those who do not harm others, who do good and are involved in various volunteering activities, and who are there for whomever needs them. These people are usually generous with their time and money. They are not troublemakers and they avoid conflict. They don't talk ill of others and have the best interests of their fellowmen at heart. The reason is these *good* people have good hearts. So, why would Jesus say in Luke 18:19, "No one is good except God alone."

We can find the answer in Psalm 14:3: "They have all turned aside; together they have become corrupt; there is none who does good, not even one." The reason is obvious in Romans 3:23 – we have all sinned.

When attending funerals, it is common to hear remarks about what a wonderful person he or she was while still alive, and many people believe that there must be a place reserved in heaven for such a good person. Sadly, this is a deception. No one can earn their place in heaven through their goodness.

We are all born as sinners. All our good intentions that lead to good deeds may count a lot in the world's eyes, but sadly, to enter heaven, it counts for nothing. It does not mean that good deeds to others are not beneficial, but it will always come from a sinful heart. There is not one human that is not carrying the seed of sin within.

If we want to be honest by analysing the good we do for others, we may be shocked to realise that the underlying motivation was not always as pure as it seemed on the surface, or that our intentions could even be in the long run to benefit ourselves – maybe to be seen, to get the admiration of others, or just to be a people pleaser. Sin clouds our good deeds.

Fortunately, God provided a way through Jesus' goodness to make us good and for our good deeds to count before God. Jesus paid the ultimate price because His goodness to us led Him to the cross. Our good deeds are the fruit we bear because we believe in the One who is without sin. By accepting Him as our Saviour, we receive His righteousness, which makes us good in His eyes already here on earth, and acceptable to His Kingdom.

"For by grace you have been saved through faith. And this is not your own doing; it is the gift of God, not a result of works, so that no one may boast." (Ephesians 2:8)

**REFLECTION: John 15:1-17**

_____
_____
_____
_____
_____
_____

# 32
# Going to Hell

One cold winter's evening, a ten-year-old girl, who stayed over for the night, and I were snuggly underneath the bedcovers reading and talking about what salvation means, when she suddenly shot upright and with great concern asked, "So my dad will go to hell, because he does not know about God. What about my mum who already died?"

This remark pulled on my heartstrings, because more often it is the parents who are concerned for their unbelieving children, but here was a ten-year-old close to tears for her lost parents, alive or dead.

The girl assumed her dad does not know about Jesus, but in this day and age there are few people in the Western world who can say they have never heard about Jesus, even if they just use the name as a swear word.

In the story of Lazarus and the rich man, it shows that some do not want to know about salvation (Luke 16). Even if someone could return from death to warn them, nothing will change their opinion. They had all the opportunities here on earth to accept Jesus, but declined any invitation.

There are many excuses, like "It is not for me," or "I am not interested," or "The Bible is a boring book, and anyway I believe it can't be trusted," or "My parents spoon-fed me too much religion," or "I'll take my chances, even if I go to hell," or "If God is a God of love, then surely He will not allow one person go to hell."

These are all lies planted in people's minds by the devil, who takes great pleasure in deceiving people to cause separation from God. It started in the Garden of Eden when Eve believed the first lie to be told, and she and Adam eagerly reacted to it. This led to the fall of humankind. Exactly what Satan wanted. His deceptions have not changed throughout the centuries. Lies are his strongest weapon. No wonder he is called the father of lies (John 8:44).

Sadly, this let many of us suffer from grieving hearts for a child, a parent, a relative, a friend who openly believes these lies. Often, our efforts to let them see the truth leads to crumbling relationships. So, what is the answer? Must we step aside and allow them to be lost for the Kingdom of God?

Yes, and no. In all cases, we need to trust the Lord. We need to remember that He has a plan for every person; God knows everyone, and he knows everything about that person, as we read in Psalm 139. He knows the deceptions. He knows how Satan blinds people against the truth. Even if the devil blinds them to the truth of the Bible, creation still reveals the existence and greatness of God.

We can't force unbelievers to see the truth or give them faith. But yes, we can help them by praying and to always be ready to tell them about the hope we have in Christ, even if they don't acknowledge God's existence as it is being revealed in creation. May we be the reason they have no excuse on judgement day, because we as believers revealed Jesus by being imitators of Him (Ephesians 5:1-2). Because of that, unbelievers won't be able to say, "I never knew Him."

Let us be persistent in prayer for the lost. It is never too late to be saved, even on one's deathbed. "For everyone that calls on the name of the Lord will be saved." (Romans 10:13)

**REFLECTION: John 8:42-47**

# 33
# Receptive Minds

During a visit to one of my daughters, I experienced a touching moment. These moments are not uncommon when grandparents visit and see how the young minds of their grandchildren are developing.

One evening after dinner, my pre-school granddaughter and six-year-old grandson eagerly wanted to repeat a psalm their parents taught them. I expected to hear Psalm 23, but to my astonishment, it was Psalm 111. They knew it all by heart. Naturally, the sweet younger sibling was being led by her brother. It warmed my heart to listen to them. It filled me with great gratitude for their Christian upbringing.

Many adults who grew up in Christian homes had to memorise Scripture as part of family devotions and Sunday School. But I wonder how many adults can still recall those scripture verses. It was like homework. You learned it by heart, each week another one, but forgot it before you must memorise the following verse.

Then there is the knowledge gained from the Bible. As children, we all loved the stories from the Old Testament. So do those who still have the privilege of attending church, Sunday School, or share in family devotions. Those are the stories we never forget.

But is it only knowledge that counts? As adults, we should make the knowledge gained from the Bible personal. How well do we know the whole Bible? Do we realise that the Old and New Testament are in unison? It is not two different individual books. It is not each with its own message.

I simplified it to my students by saying the Old Testament predicts and is full of promises that point to the coming of a Messiah. With the birth of Jesus Christ as the Messiah, the New Testament fulfils those predictions and promises.

The Old and New Testament are interconnected. The one can't be read without the other in mind. To read the Bible just for the sake of reading material that is interesting and to gain knowledge for the sake of knowledge, will do little to help us to grow in our faith. Proverbs 2 describes how we should seek growth in knowledge of the Scriptures. This will lead us to "understand the fear of the Lord and find the knowledge of God." (Proverbs 2:5)

It requires discipline to read the Bible daily. Life and its busyness take over easily. Personally, I found that setting a specific time aside helps to keep to reading the Bible. One or two chapters of a book are better than skipping the reading altogether. A Study Bible is always an excellent investment too. There are many books and websites with suggestions for keeping notes if you are a person who likes to keep a journal.

From this routine, a desire should follow to memorise Bible verses. Many years ago, I read a story that made a lifelong impression on me. It was about a missionary who was in prison because of his faith. The authorities took his Bible. But he knew so many Bible verses by heart that he felt God's presence continually, regardless of his horrible surroundings and treatment. It is an amazing experience when the Holy Spirit reminds us at the very perfect moment of a verse when we need it for ourselves or to help others.

May we be able to say, "I have stored up your word in my heart, that I might not sin against you." (Psalm 119:11)

**REFLECTION: Psalm 119:18**

___
___
___
___
___
___

## 34
## What is your Reality?

During a session with a group of late-primary school youths, I asked them to tell me the difference between fiction and non-fiction. They had no problem explaining the difference. But when I asked for an example to illustrate the difference, one boy got very agitated. He insisted that a TV series that was running for decades was not fiction at all.

In tears, he blurted out, "You say fiction is not real or even true, but I tell you all those actors are actual people, and the episodes are all true."

The rest of the boys were speechless that this timid, shy boy could get so upset about something that they knew very well was not real.

This made me think about a conversation I had with an unbeliever who had studied theology and then turned away from the faith. One of his remarks at the time was, and I quote, "What is reality? It is only what we can see, touch, smell, and hear. Therefore, religion is not for me. Everything about it is unseen. You believe in an unseen God that works in unseen ways and so forth. Living day by day, that is reality. So, I create my own reality."

But that is what makes the Christian faith so extraordinary. Faith is not an object which can be touched, smelled, heard or seen, but every believer will agree that faith is just as real to us as oxygen, unseen by the eye, but without it we can't be alive.

Faith is "the assurance of things hoped for, the conviction of things not seen." (Hebrews 11:1) If hope was an object that could be obtained, it would be lifeless and worthless. Romans 8:24 puts it so clearly, "For in this hope we were saved. Now hope that is seen is not hope. For who hopes for what he sees?"

Faith is unseen by the eye, but it does not mean faith does not exist or that it results from believers' imaginations. Faith comes from God. "No one has ever seen God; the only God, who is at the Father's side, he has made him known." (John 1:18) He made Himself known in our hearts by the faith we receive from Him. With faith comes also understanding. Hebrews 11:3 says, "By faith we understand that the universe was created by the word of God, so that what is seen was not made of things that are visible."

The Old Testament stories are a wonderful gift that we should cherish. They have the same suspense as a work of fiction, but reveal the true nature of our unseen God. Therefore, God becomes real in this life amid the earthly reality we share. An earthly reality where non-believers try to remove any reminders of an unseen God as a possible reality.

Believers and unbelievers must share the reality of living on this planet in the here and now. But if you believe this is the only reality, and if your reality will end with dying, then you are to be pitied.

Followers of Christ believe whole-heartedly the reality that awaits us after death. Departing from earth to heaven can never be comparable. 1 Corinthians 2:9 assures us, "But, as it is written, "What no eye has seen, nor ear heard, nor the heart of man imagined, what God has prepared for those who love him."

It should strengthen our faith daily knowing that we are only passersby in this life, for it is not even close to the reality that awaits us after we passed on. "But our citizenship is in heaven, and from it we await a Savior, the Lord Jesus Christ, who will transform our lowly body to be like his glorious body, by the power that enables him even to subject all things to himself." (Philippians 3:20-21)

**REFLECTION: Revelation 22:1-5          Revelation 7:9-17**

_____
_____
_____
_____
_____
_____

# 35
# Rejoice

Part of my weekly schedule in teaching Bible in Schools was to take a class at a small two-teacher school in the country. They were lovely, unspoiled children between the ages of eight to eleven-year-olds.

One of the worship songs the students loved to sing was based on Psalm 118:24, "This is the day the Lord has made; let us rejoice and be glad in it." They sang it with great enthusiasm. The melody is jubilant and the students' enjoyment in singing the song was contagious. Looking at their cheerful faces and listening to them filled me with pure joy.

These words in Psalm 118:24 can have various interpretations, but considering the joyful expressions of the children, I would gladly embrace the interpretation that today is the day to be glad.

Part of being a child is to live in the moment, and for them it was to be happy today because God gave them that day to be happy. But in a more matured way, the reasons for adults to rejoice in this very day have different aspects of it.

To wake up to a new day, knowing that the Lord created that day and is going to fill it with opportunity upon opportunity to serve Him, provides ample reasons to rejoice. Each day given to us shines like a beautiful white pearl. On its own, it doesn't seem much worth but add to it day by day another pearl and it becomes a beautiful, treasured piece of jewellery when strung together.

Thankfulness is the key word here. The realisation that you are alive and, by God's grace, receive new mercies for that day, is enough reason to rejoice. In doing so, we answer to Philippians 4:4, "Rejoice in the Lord always; again I will say, rejoice."

All of us experience days when we wake up and do not feel that well physically. Some mornings we may feel mentally exhausted by just thinking ahead of the day and all our commitments. Those days are the ones where we need to turn our attention deliberately back to the blessings we receive daily. It is good reminding ourselves of the words in Lamentations 3:22-23, "The steadfast love of the Lord never ceases, his mercies never come to an end; they are new every morning; great is your faithfulness."

David realised the importance of focusing on God before the day started, "when I remember you upon my bed, and meditate on you in the watches of the night; for you have been my help and in the shadow of your wings I will sing for joy." (Psalm 63:6-7) Surely, after a night like that, by dawn break David got out of bed with joy in his heart.

But we can't rejoice in today and see it as a new day that God created if we have not accepted Jesus as our Saviour. Paul writes in 2 Corinthians 6:2, "For he says, 'In a favorable time I listened to you, and in a day of salvation I have helped you.' Behold, now is the favorable time; behold now is the day of salvation."

Therefore, there is no better day than today that can lead to salvation. Sadly, there are those who believe in the existence of God but never see it necessary or relevant to give their lives to Him. They may even think it is not the time now, but maybe later. To them, the day of salvation may never come and with it the rejoicing of becoming a child of God. Accepting Jesus gives a different meaning to waking up to a new day, created by God for us to rejoice in his love and with a heart overflowing with thankfulness.

Today is the day. "Today, if you hear his voice, do not harden your hearts as in the rebellion." (Hebrews 3:15)

**REFLECTION: Psalm 107:1-22**

# 36
# Words and Actions

Being a facilitator for different programmes for students with behavioural problems, their remarks often took me by surprise. During one of these sessions, I mentioned that the Bible often compares God to being a loving parent. A few sneered. Of course, I wanted to know why.

The following were the answers I got: "My parents are not loving, my mum always yells at me," and "My dad never seems impressed with my school report. It doesn't matter how well I do. It is never good enough."

The remarks continued. "Why would anyone compare God to a parent?" "I don't feel loved in the way my parents talk to me." Another remarked, "My Dad does not act as if he loves me."

Imagine children experiencing such attitudes daily. What a lifelong imprint it leaves on such a child's soul. These attitudes plant the seeds in their childhood years, making them believe they are not worthy to be loved. They are not good enough.

The saddest aspect is that their belief system is already based on negativity. This is especially true when they hear God's word. If the important grown-ups in their lives didn't treat them well and they never felt loved, could God really love them?

It is easy to say, because we are believers, we will treat our children well. We raise them in a Christian church and give them a Christian upbringing. But is that a guarantee? Why do many Christian youths struggle with behaviour?

I am convinced not all Christian parents are practising what they preach. Often it is only lip service. It's possible that their parents' actions and behaviour towards them have prevented them themselves of knowing how to show love. Unfortunately, they did not learn to trust their parents. Now their own children don't trust them because of their behaviour towards them. Unloving actions and speech can be emotionally devastating.

Jesus is very clear about the responsibility of parents. "Whoever receives one such child in my name receives me, but whoever causes one of these little ones who believe in me to sin, it would be better for him to have a great millstone fastened around his neck and to be drowned in the depth of the sea." (Matthew 18:6)

Children are precious in the Lord's sight. Let our actions and words bring Him glory and honour. Your example will influence a child not only in the present but will leave a lifelong imprint on them. Many times it plays a major role in the path they take later in life.

It is never too late when we realise we have hurt a child through our unloving speech or actions, even if it happened a long time ago. Humbling yourself before the Lord is the first step in breaking this cycle. Acknowledge our sin before Him, repent and ask Him for forgiveness.

Ask that child's forgiveness. Forgive those who hurt you and whose actions led to your hurtful behaviour. Avoid the blame game to justify your actions. Colossians 3:13-14 puts it so well, "…bearing with one another and, if one has a complaint against another, forgiving each other; as the Lord has forgiven you, so you also must forgive. And above all these put on love, which binds everything together in perfect harmony."

**REFLECTION: Colossians 3:20-25        Proverbs 3:1-5**

_____
_____
_____
_____
_____
_____

# 37
# Favouritism

Different students at different times asked me if God has favourites. When I asked what makes them think that is the case, they would say that there is always a favoured one. One told me, "My sister is a favourite of my mum's." When I asked why, the answer was, "My mother often surprises my sister with clothes, but not me. She says I don't need it, which is not true." Another boy chimed in, saying, "My dad takes my brother fishing, but when I ask to go, he says I'd be a nuisance."

Favouritism is not a modern phenomenon but it was very real in the Bible. In the Book of Genesis, we read Abraham favoured Isaac over Ishmael. This is understandable because Abraham conceived Ishmael with Hagar, the slave that Sarah gave Abraham for that purpose. Sarah, his beloved wife, became later the mother of Isaac. We saw it continue with Isaac, who favoured Esau over Jacob. Esau was a man who loved hunting and being in the field, like his father. It then continued with Jacob, who favoured Joseph over his other sons. Joseph was the firstborn of Rachel, whom Jacob loved and whom he favoured over Lea, his other wife.

These examples of favouritism in the Bible did not lead to good outcomes. The same will be today. Isaac and Ishmael became enemies, and so did Jacob and Esau. Joseph's brothers tried to kill him, changed their minds and sold him to Egyptian merchants.

Favouritism in any form, situation, or of any kind is unacceptable, unjustified and unkind. It hurts others. It could lead to hostility, jealousy, even hatred, a sense of unworthiness. You don't need to be a child to experience favouritism – it is just as common among adults.

You often hear the remark that life is not fair. Is it life that is not fair or is it the unfairness caused by people? The wealthy, the famous, the beautiful, the genius, and the achiever are all favoured over the poor, the oppressed, and the disadvantaged.

But favouritism or partiality is not God's way. In the Book of James, we read, "My brothers, show no partiality as you hold the faith in our Lord Jesus Christ, the Lord of glory." (James 2:1) It is a sin to put some above others. "But if you show partiality, you are committing sin and are convicted by the law as transgressors." (James 2:9) "If you really fulfill the royal law according to the Scripture, 'You shall love your neighbour as yourself,' you are doing well." (James 2:8)

Under God's guidance, we should treat all people in love and fairness. Kindness, gentleness, and a heart that overflows with empathy for others is the example Jesus set. He strongly acted against the partiality of the religious leaders, even opposing them with strong words. They put themselves above the people and even above God with senseless laws and rules. This is still happening in all spheres of life. It causes a great deal of suffering for those who are on the receiving end.

We are all sinners and therefore can't say we have never shown partiality or favoured any person over another. Let us look at Jesus, the perfect example of impartiality. He came to save all those who turn to Him. His suffering on the cross became the bridge that leads to eternal life.

"Truly I understand that God shows no partiality, but in every nation anyone who fears him and does what is right is acceptable to Him." (Acts 10:34)

**REFLECTION: Galatians 3:23-29**

_____
_____
_____
_____
_____
_____
_____

# 38
# Discipline versus Punishment

South Africa must have been one of the last countries to allow television. That happened in 1975. My husband and I, with a growing family, were considering whether to undertake such an enormous expense. In the meantime, the elderly couple next door graciously invited our seven-year-old son over. He could watch a popular children's programme at their home regularly. It lasted only fifteen minutes, and he was supposed to return straight home afterwards. One specific evening he came home an hour late.

His disobedience displeased us, but before we could reprimand him, he interjected, "I know I did wrong and I'm sorry. I know I deserve a spanking because that helps me to become a good grown-up. Also, you told me the Bible tells parents to do that if a child does not obey. So that is okay. You can spank me now."

He obviously had taken on board our explanations for discipline when being disobedient. But did he see it as being disciplined or punished? Hopefully, not the latter. With punishment there is often a lack of compassion, an element of condemnation, and a short-term goal. Whereas with discipline it is to instruct, to train that person to change in behaviour. Over time, that will be beneficial to himself and to all who cross his path.

Right through the Old and New Testaments we read about God disciplining His people, but also about his punishment to those who rebelled against Him.

Everyone who believes that Jesus died for his/her sin, becomes an adopted child of God. Just as parents discipline children so does God, our heavenly Father, discipline us. We would rather avoid being disciplined, but the result always brings us a step closer to becoming Christlike. As Hebrews 12:11 points out, "For the moment all discipline seems painful rather than pleasant, but later it yields the peaceful fruit of righteousness to those who have been trained by it."

An example of a Bible figure who was disciplined is David. Saul relentlessly pursued him, which God allowed in His providence. David's trust and faith in God grew through those trials. No reader of Psalms can deny the depth of David's love for God.

Another example is Joseph. All the hardship he went through after being sold to the Egyptian merchants prepared him to become second in charge of Pharaoh's kingdom. In both Bible characters' trials, there was no element of punishment. God's aim was to teach them about Himself, to be trusted and worshipped, so they could experience how much He had in store for them. Also to be refined like gold. Sanctified to His glory.

Regarding the punishment aspect, we see many biblical examples of punishment. God punished individuals, and the Jews as a whole, for rebelling against Him. Their acts deserved punishment. We learn about only one undeserved punishment – that which came upon the Lord, Jesus Christ. He, without sin, paid the full price by receiving punishment for our sins, though we deserved that punishment. "He himself bore our sins in his body on the tree, that we might die to sin and live to righteousness. By his wounds you have been healed." (1 Peter 2:24)

Let the words of Hebrews 10:29 drive our compassion for the lost, "How much worse punishment, do you think, will be deserved by the one who has trampled underfoot the Son of God …"

**REFLECTION: Isaiah 53:1-12**

## 39
## Keeps on Escaping

Once I overheard a mother saying how her eight-year-old enjoyed a church camp. She smiled tenderly and said, "Lizzie's first words upon arriving home were, "Mummy, I gave my heart to Jesus."

The mother continued telling how she reminded her daughter that she did the same thing the year before at another church camp. Lizzie agreed but admitted that Jesus keeps on escaping.

I am sure many of us can relate to the fact that after we invited Jesus into our lives or, as Lizzie put it, gave our hearts to Jesus, the awareness of His presence waned. It may feel as if He disappeared. Maybe it happened after we attended a conference, camp, or any other meetings with fellow brothers and sisters in the faith. We may have been moved deeply by the Holy Spirit's presence. Returning to our usual environment and the mundane of everyday life may lead to a feeling that the Lord had escaped. But during those gatherings, there is often a heightening of emotions. It takes some time to adjust to everyday life after these experiences. Realising He is just as much present in the mundane may take some time. This is understandable.

But there are many of us who felt at some stage of our lives that Jesus had escaped. The result is that we lose easily our desire to stay in the Word. Our prayers start to feel repetitive and our enthusiasm for church attendance and for other fellowship gatherings decreases. We may continue as if nothing has changed, but to be honest, we may feel we have lost Him. Satan deceives us into thinking He left us and in believing the lie; this weakens our faith. Losing our sense of belonging and being not aware anymore of His love cause despair and even depression.

Most important is to realise that our faith does not rest on feelings but on knowledge. The knowledge that Jesus is unchangeable. "Jesus Christ is the same yesterday, and today, and forever." (Hebrews 13:8)

Therefore, Jesus does not move away from us, but we move away from Him. The promise in verse 5 confirms this: He will never leave us nor forsake us.

Maybe there is a sin we committed, which we don't want to admit even to ourselves. This prevents us from confessing to the Lord and asking His forgiveness. David felt separated from God after He sinned with Bathsheba. In Psalm 51, we read about David's sincere confession and the restoration of his relationship with God. We may not have sinned as gravely as David. It may be any sin that we stubbornly hang on to.

Another reason may be that the cares of life take over and there is no time left to spend with the Lord, even giving Him any thought. With all the daily commitments, heightened stress levels and anxiety that goes with them, there is just no space for the Lord. We may think attending church services on a Sunday is enough. With our lives depending on our own planning, we easily forget Jesus' words of "…apart from me, you can do nothing." (John 15:5)

A Puritan once wrote in his writings that the busier the day ahead is going to be, the longer He spends in prayer before he meets the day head-on. By having Jesus day by day as the most important priority in our lives, there is no need to fear His escaping. It all starts with what is happening between you and the Lord in private.

Jesus' words are just as relevant today as when He told his disciples, "But when you pray, go into your room and shut the door and pray to your Father who is in secret. And your Father who sees in secret will reward you."

**REFLECTION: John 15:1-11**

_____
_____
_____
_____
_____
_____
_____

# 40
# No Grandchildren

I recall with joy in my heart the day our granddaughter confirmed her faith. Confidently, she stood behind the lectern facing the congregation that morning, presenting her testimony. She shared with a glowing face the reason behind her decision to commit herself to the Lord.

"I grew up in a Christian home, attended a Christian school, and had Christian friends all around me. I felt my heart was right with God. Why not? My parents follow and love the Lord, so naturally I was His child too. But recently at a church camp, the leader pointed out that God has no grandchildren. It was an eye opener, and I realised this was very personal. My faith rests not on the credentials of my parents but is between God and me alone."

The church environment, a Christian home, and exposure to people sharing similar Christian values and worldviews, as well as upbringing by believing parents, pose an enormous danger. It becomes easily a blurring of identity. The focus is often not on Christ Himself. The question, "What is my personal relationship regarding Him?" hardly ever comes to mind.

Regular churchgoers know the way of salvation. We know that Jesus' death on the cross atoned for our sins, setting us free from punishment; Jesus dying for us made us right with God. His resurrection on the third day made it possible for us to have victory over death. We can look forward to eternal life with Him.

This is the foundation of the Christian faith. But often, faith rests on knowledge only. For many, that is enough. They are content to live life as it is without desire or even realising there is so much more than what knowledge can offer. They remain spiritually untouched. The Lord wants us to experience in this life a foretaste of what's awaiting us in His Kingdom. That can only happen if we open the gates of our innermost hearts to Him.

Our Father in heaven desires to have an intimate relationship with us. If you are a parent, you will know how disappointing it is and even hurtful if your children are aloof and avoid sharing things with you. In times like that, it doesn't change the fact that they are your children and you are the parents, but their behaviour changes the dynamics of the relationship. Whatever they do or say, however upsetting or discerning it may be, the love and compassion of the parent will always continue.

That we become children of God is undeniably clear in this verse, "See what kind of love the Father has given to us, that we should be called children of God; and so we are." (1 John 3:1)

However, though God created us, we are not born as His children; His grace chooses us to accept the Lord's salvation, and only then do we become His children. Ephesians 1:4-5 confirms our adoption into God's family, "...even as he chose us in him before the foundation of the world, that we should be holy and blameless before him. In love he predestined us for adoption to himself as sons [daughters] through Jesus Christ."

Jesus' words in John 14:21 illustrates our loving relationship with the Father, but also the obedience that goes with it, "Whoever has my commandments and keeps them, he it is who loves me. And he who loves me will be loved by my Father, and I will love him and manifest myself to him."

**REFLECTION: Ephesians 5:1,13-21**

# THE AUTHOR'S NOTES

Throughout my life, children from all ages, including young adults and my own children, enriched my life. I shared in their joy and in their pain. I realised early on that I had a gift for understanding children's hearts. Probably because I grew up in an environment where there was a great lack of insight and understanding of me as a child.

Therefore, when I was contemplating writing a devotional book, the idea came to me to use the biblical views and remarks of the young people. These became a building stone for the rest of each devotion. I thank the Lord, who led me by the Spirit to make this a reality and who inspired me to approach each devotion in this way. He blessed my memory, for sure, to recall all these moments.

Children had a special place during Jesus' ministry on earth. The Bible frequently likens Christians to children. The most comforting assurance is that we become beloved children of God through the grace to believe in the risen Christ. Our faith gives us access to become adopted children of the Father and to receive an inheritance far beyond this world.

Why only 40 devotionals? There are two reasons for that: I could not recall over 40 remarks or views biblically connected that would be suitable and, second, 40 is a very significant number throughout the Bible.

I trust these devotions will be a tender reminder of to whom you belong. If you are still in doubt, I pray you will reflect prayerfully to step out in faith and become a beloved child of God.

May I add it is of utmost importance to spend time with God daily. Spending time with God will yield a joyful and meaningful life, multiplied many times over. A life that will honour and glorify Him.

Copies of this book can be ordered direct from Lorraine **if you are in New Zealand:** anjo.books@gmx.com

Otherwise, you may order from any online store, worldwide.

www.ingramcontent.com/pod-product-compliance
Lightning Source LLC
Chambersburg PA
CBHW062042290426
44109CB00026B/2703